THE PROBLEM OF SPACE
IN JEWISH MEDIAEVAL
PHILOSOPHY

COLUMBIA UNIVERSITY ORIENTAL STUDIES
Vol. XI

THE PROBLEM OF SPACE IN JEWISH MEDIAEVAL PHILOSOPHY

BY

ISRAEL ISAAC EFROS

AMS PRESS, INC.
NEW YORK, N.Y. 10003
1966

Copyright 1917
Columbia University Press

Reprinted with the
permission of the original publisher

AMS PRESS, INC.
NEW YORK, N.Y. 10003
1966

Manufactured in the United States of America

NOTE

IN the ordinary treatises dealing with philosophical problems the effort expended towards their solution by the Jewish philosophers of the Middle Ages is accorded a very small space. This is due to two causes. The writings of these thinkers are not always and readily accessible in translations, and those scholars who are acquainted with their writings at first hand have failed to put forward the views they have expressed upon these problems. It is, therefore, with pleasure that I present the following exposition of one of them—that of Space—as that subject was discussed in Jewish circles during the Middle Ages; and especially as Dr. Efros submits their standpoint as a possible solution of the vexed question.

RICHARD GOTTHEIL.

Nov. 15, 1916.

IN MEMORY OF MY DEAR SISTER
ROSE
WHO PASSED AWAY IN THE BLOOM OF LIFE
THIS IS SORROWFULLY DEDICATED

CONTENTS

	PAGE
INTRODUCTION	1

CHAPTER I

EMPIRICAL SPACE	22
I. Space and Spirit	22
II. Space and Matter	32
III. Infinite Divisibility	46

CHAPTER II

ABSOLUTE SPACE	61
I. Space versus Place	63
II. The Void	71

CHAPTER III

INFINITE SPACE	88
CONCLUSION	110

APPENDIX

GLOSSARY OF SOME HEBREW PHILOSOPHICAL TERMS IN CONNEXION WITH THE SUBJECT OF SPACE	117
INDEX	123

THE PROBLEM OF SPACE IN JEWISH MEDIAEVAL PHILOSOPHY

I TRUST that the term 'Jewish Philosophy' does not require any apology; indeed, I should owe the reader a greater apology were I to attempt to give any. The famous or infamous indictment of Renan[1] that the Jews are destitute of any philosophic talent is best refuted by expository works which bring to light the depths of Jewish thought. The refutation was begun by Solomon Munk, and is still continued by every monograph that has appeared on the subject. As far as the problem of space is concerned, a problem that has baffled human thought ever since the days of Zeno of Elea, I hope that the subsequent pages will serve as a testimony of Jewish profoundness of thought and Jewish comprehensiveness of the grave antinomies that this difficult problem presents.

The scope of this work is limited, as the title indicates, to Mediaeval Jewish Philosophy, i.e. to that epoch in Jewish thought which was inaugurated by Isaac Israeli of Kairwan, an older contemporary of Saadya, and culminated in Don Isaac Abrabanel—a period of five centuries least familiar to the general student of philosophy, but which produced the choicest fruits of the maturing Jewish intellect. I am aware of the abundance of ideas relative to the problem of space which are harboured in the Talmudic and Midrashic literature; but their influence on

---

[1] See his *Histoire des langues sémitiques*, I, 1.

the philosophy of the period under discussion is, as far as our problem is concerned, of no great importance, and is therefore omitted. For a similar reason I shall not deal here with Philo's views on space,[2] or, on the other side, with the views of Spinoza and others, especially our great contemporaries Hermann Cohen and Henri Bergson. Nevertheless, should the reader resent the limitations that the term 'Mediaeval' imposes, I shall attempt some day to resume the discussion and deal with those views that are here out of place.

INTRODUCTION

I. On the surface, the idea of space is comparatively simple and intelligible. It is the idea of extensity of things, the idea of an external world that is not a mere pin-point, all the parts of which being coalesced and compressed to form a non-magnitudinal and indivisible unity, but stretched out and extended around us, all the parts of which are lying *side by side* of one another, and thus capable of being measured. We perceive this extensity of things and the 'alongsidedness' of its parts, by our visual and tactual and muscular senses. When we move our eye to circumspect a landscape, we have a sense of its range or extensiveness. When we lay our hand over this desk, we have a sense of a greater area than when we lay our hand over a pin-point. And when we furthermore move our hand so as to describe a circle, we feel a vastness around us. And now when we gather our perceptions of extended objects, and employ the method of generalization and abstraction, we arrive at

[2] As for Philo's views on space, the reader may find something in Leisegang's *Die Raumtheorie im späteren Platonismus* (Weida i. Th.: Thomas & Hubert, 1911), but the account is by no means satisfactory.

the concept of extensity occupied or not occupied by concrete objects—the concept of pure space.

Yet when we come to analyse this common conception of space we find ourselves beset with puzzling problems and baffling antinomies. The notion of space, I said, lies in the alongsidedness of parts. But those parts themselves in order to be perceived must be composed of smaller parts, and so on; since the perception of any extended quantity involves a perception of parts. But what of the tiniest speck, the *minimum sensibile*, in which no parts seem to be present; how is it possibly perceived? And if that is true, every body is composed of an infinite number of particles, or, in other words, every finite object around us, from the mountain height to the grain of sand, is really infinite. Thus an ant moving over a blade of grass is moving over an infinite, and when you have moved over from one corner of the room to the other, you have completed an infinite series of points. All of which is absurd.

Leaving the question whether space is infinite in division, we may ask whether space is infinite in extent. We conceive a thing when we know it or seem to know it definitely, while infinity carries with it an indefinite and indeterminate element, which admits of no conception. A definite knowledge of a thing implies the ability to compare it to others and distinguish it from others. But the infinite is incomparable and indistinguishable. Yet, on the other hand, if space is finite and bounded, the question is: By what is it bounded? What is beyond its boundary? And what if a thing were to be carried beyond the realm of space; would it shrink into nothingness?

One more question: Is space itself material or immaterial? It could not be material, for a thing could not occupy another unyielding material thing without violating the law of impenetrability. If immaterial, what is it? What is meant by an immaterial something existing in the external world? Perhaps it is not an external reality. Perhaps it is a mere mental illusion, one of those illusions with which the mind is wont to deceive mankind. But is it conceivable that the objective reality is unspatial, that it has no magnitude whatsoever, that this vast universe with its stars and planets is really a mere geometrical point located nowhere except in the mind of the mathematician? If space is an illusion, why cannot the elephant escape through the key-hole? To make space mental does not make matters more conceivable.

Such are the difficulties which present themselves in connexion with the notion of space. The deeper the mind delves into the problem, the greater the tangle. It is one of the sphinxes in the deserts of thought. From the dawn of speculation we find space to be one of the most prominent objects of investigation; Zeno, Plato, and Aristotle bent their great intellects on the solution of space; colossal systems of science were reared on the notion of space. Yet the meaning of space has remained a mystery till the present day. Indeed, the difficulties seem to increase with the time.

It would be preposterous of course to claim that the Jews were cognizant of all these difficulties that the modern era has introduced. If we turn to examine the views on space maintained by the two greatest of Greek thinkers, who had such an enormous influence on Jewish thought, we will get a notion of the type of problems that we will have to deal with in the following chapters. In addition, it will present us the sources and the starting-point for the views that are to be discussed in this study.

Plato's Conception of Space

II. Students of Plato are not in agreement as to his view on space. Some maintain that in Plato's conception space is the primaeval matter, the original substrate which was fashioned by the Demiurgus into all perceptible objects, that it is the raw material out of which the great artisan created all things. In support of this interpretation they fall back upon Aristotle, who in his *Physics*, IV, 4 remarks as follows: 'Hence also Plato in the *Timaeus* says that matter and a receptacle are the same thing. For that which is capable of receiving and a receptacle are the same thing.' Thus Aristotle makes Plato—and who would understand Plato better than his illustrious disciple?—identify space with matter, pre-existing and receiving all created things. Hence also all mediaeval philosophers unanimously assumed that Plato affirmed the eternity of matter. On the other hand, there are many scholars who claim that Aristotle misunderstood Plato, and that according to the latter space and matter are not identical, but two distinct and separate beings.[3]

Now, in favour of the former view, the following arguments are generally adduced. Plato speaking about the third γένος, the abiding substrate in the incessant mutation of phenomena, compares it to the gold that is moulded into all sorts of figures, to the wax that is impressed by the seal.[4] The elements, fire, air, water, earth, are not four varieties of Being, four different essences, but mere states or modes of one sensuous mass. 'Fire is that part of her nature which from time to time is inflamed, and

---

[3] For a detailed bibliography of the two views, see Zeller's *Plato and the Older Academy*, ch. VII, notes 18, 20, and also his *Platonische Studien*, 212, 222.
[4] *Tim.*, p. 50.

water that which is moistened, and that the molten substance becomes earth and air in so far as she receives the impressions.'[5] Evidently Plato had in mind a sensuous ground-work of all existence. Besides, it would be inconceivable to reduce all things to an incorporeal essence or mere space. Plato, it is true, characterizes the four elements according to geometrical solids consisting of nothing but triangular surfaces.[6] Zeller points out this latter Platonic theory as a decisive proof against the theory of corporeal primary matter.[7] But when Plato maintained that 'every solid must necessarily be contained in planes', he did not mean that they are *composed* of planes and nothing else. He did not mean to reduce this solid world to an empty geometrical structure, to a mere house of cards. A thousand planes do not make an actual solid. But it seems that Zeller here lost the thread of Plato's argument. Up to the middle of p. 53 Plato was discussing the three-fold classification of Being, and particularly the material substrate of all things, that indeterminate mass existing before the creation, in which 'fire and water and earth and air had only certain faint traces of themselves, and were altogether such as everything might be expected to be in the absence of God'.[8] And now Plato commences a description of the process of creation proper, the process of formation of the universe. I mean, putting form to the primordial chaotic matter and unfolding its dormant elements.[9] And it is here in the discussion of the formal

---

[5] *Tim.*, p. 51. [6] *Ibid.*, p. 54.
[7] Zeller, *Plato and the Older Academy*, VII.
[8] *Tim.* 51.
[9] Νῦν δ' οὖν τὴν διάταξιν αὐτῶν ἐπιχειρητέον ἑκάστων καὶ γένεσιν ἀήθει λόγῳ πρὸς ὑμᾶς δηλοῦν, *Tim.* 53 b The word *diataxis* Jowett translated by 'disposition', which may suggest that Plato sets out to discuss the essence

aspect of the universe that the description of the geometrical figures comes. Thus, things were not *made of* but *according to* plans, surfaces, and space is not the material but the formal cause of all things.[10]

To come back to our main discussion, another argument might be presented in favour of the materialistic view of space. In describing the primordial receptacle, the matter of generation, he remarks 'that if the model is to take every variety of forms, then the matter in which the model is fashioned when duly prepared, must be formless, and the forms must come from without' (*Tim.*, p. 50). Now it is conceived that Plato believed in the primordial existence of an absolutely formless mass which was informed from without like the wax by the seal. The modern man can hardly conceive matter and form being separate: this is because his accumulated experience leads him to be cautious in forming his cognitions, and not to attempt to leap over the circle of phenomena. The ancients, on the other hand, were inexperienced, youthful, rash, and ready to objectify and hypostasize any idea that presented itself to their premature minds. It is only the particularistic view of mankind, i.e. the view of man as separate

---

of things, but a more faithful rendering is 'arrangement', which fits better with the line of argument.

[10] Indeed it is highly probable that even the Pythagoreans, who held that number is the principle of all things, did not hypostasize it, did not consider it the essence and substance of things, but rather their formal element. Aristotle, in his *Metaph.*, I, 2, 5; XIV, 3 asserts that the Pythagoreans considered numbers to be things: and in *Metaph.*, I, 6 he remarks that they are prototypes of things. Zeller (see his *Greek Philosophy to the time of Socrates*, I, p. 369) lays stress on the first statement, and explains that they are also prototypes in the sense of law, but many other students of ancient philosophy support the latter statement of Aristotle to the exclusion of the former. See Ritter, *Geschichte der alten Philosophie*, IV, ch. 2.

individuals, that makes Socrates and Plato ancient; a truer view is the general and evolutionary one which considers John Locke and Immanuel Kant as ancient, and Socrates and Plato as youths wantoning with abstractions and mere ideas. Plato particularly had that tendency to objectify and to hypostasize logical realities. One can therefore easily grasp Plato's assumption of the coalescing of two independent elemental realities, form and matter thus producing all things. But one cannot conceive how Plato would make empty space as the universal substratum and at the same time insist that the form should come from without. For if form here means anything, it means certain limitations of magnitude. This body has a cubical form, another spherical and still another oval. But magnitude means extension, and to speak of formless space is to speak of an unextended space or of a non-spatial space, which is absurd.[11] And it is equally absurd to insist on having the form come from without, for by definition form can come from space only.[12]

So much for the corporealistic view of Plato's conception of space. On the other hand, Plato also speaks of space in a manner that entirely excludes all notions of corporeality. He defines it in the *Tim.* 52 as the 'home for all created things'. By 'created things' one naturally understands concrete objects composed of matter and form; and Plato

[11] It is impossible to evade the argument by reading into Plato Aristotle's definition of form, λόγος τῆς οὐσίας. The analogies that Plato finds to Form in the seal impress on the wax and in the transient shapes of the gold, obviate such an interpretation.

[12] Perhaps a similar objection can be raised against formless matter, but we must not forget that the doctrine that extension constitutes the very *essence* of material things was not yet fully realized in the days of Plato. The Atomists, for example, believed in material atoms which were at the same time invisible.

defines space as outside of them, as their home. Space then, according to Plato, must be immaterial. Furthermore, he maintains that this third nature 'is eternal, and admits not of destruction' (p. 52). Now in p. 28 he had laid down a rule that 'that which is apprehended by intelligence and reason is always in the same state; but that which is conceived by opinion, with the help of sensation, and without reason, is always in a process of becoming and perishing, and never really is'. In other words, things material are destructible, and things spiritual are eternal; and since space is according to Plato eternal, it cannot be corporeal.

These are the two views of the Platonic conception of space, but it seems to me that either of these two views attaches itself to one particular passage in the *Timaeus*, and does not do full justice to the argument as a whole. It seems to me that the adherent of either view tears passages out of their context, and hence arrives at such contradictory results. Hence it is of paramount importance to analyse very carefully the whole development of the argument. But first let me point out a curious and suspicious contradiction in Plato. First, it is to be noticed that from p. 49 to p. 52, where he introduced this third γένος, this 'receptacle, the matter of generation', and where he discusses it rather in detail, he does not mention even once the word space or its equivalent (χώρα, τόπος), but in p. 52 he introduces again a third γένος, and there he refers constantly to space and no longer to any 'receptacle'. Is it not curious? On further inspection, the matter becomes more interesting. In p. 52 he describes space as eternal, indestructible, 'perceived without the help of sense, by a kind of spurious reason'. Now turn to pp. 49-52, and here he never mentions that the receptacle is eternal. True, it is spoken of as 'always the same', but the expression seems to have a rather relative value. It is always the same while the images and the forms that it assumes are coming and going, transient, brief, and fleeting. It is the abiding groundwork of all transitory things. Yet he does not say that it is in itself, absolutely speaking, eternal and indestructible. Thus it is strange that the attribute of eternity, so emphatically stated with reference to space (p. 52), is entirely overlooked in the case of the receptacle (pp. 49-52).

The second characteristic of space, that it is perceived without the help of sense, by a kind of spurious reason, in a dreamlike manner, is also not clearly stated in the case of the receptacle. He describes it as 'an invisible and formless being', and is 'most comprehensible' (p. 51), and he maintains that it is known through a consideration of the fleeting images. The meaning then is clear. We cannot perceive the receptacle, for it is formless. When I direct my gaze at the tree, I do not see the thing in itself, I see the form of the tree. Only its externality is revealed to my senses. Sensation then has to do with the forms of objects, not with the objects *per se*. Hence one may naturally expect that the receptacle which is formless should not be perceptible. How then is the thing known? The answer is: the sensation of the transitory and fleeting object leads the mind to assume an abiding groundwork, a receptacle. Hence the latter is known empirically, and, strictly speaking, adhering to the Platonic terminology, we have no knowledge of space but 'right opinion', for every empirical cognition is a mere opinion. And yet, in p. 52, Plato maintains that space is known by reason, though a spurious one, and that it is not at all an empirical concept.[13]

Thus the whole matter is very puzzling. Is Plato contradicting himself in such close juxtaposition, or is the receptacle one thing and space another? If we now proceed to a general analysis of Plato's argument in the *Timaeus*, I think the puzzle will be solved.

After an invocation of the gods, Timaeus, the natural philosopher, begins the story of creation. There are two natures in the universe, Being and Becoming, the permanent and the mutable, the eternal and the destructible. Everything that was created has had a design and realizes a purpose. This idea is fully amplified and elaborated in some detail. But this represents only one view of creation, namely, that of the creator. And so at the end of p. 47 he remarks: 'Thus far in what we have been saying, with small exception, the works of intelligence have been set forth; and now we must place by the side of them the things done from necessity, for the creation is mixed and is the result of a union of necessity and mind.' If by the mind ($νοῦς$) Plato understands the rational, and the forming element, then by necessity ($ἀνάγκη$) he understands the irrational or the plastic element in creation. By $ἀνάγκη$ thus is meant the *motum non movens*, that which receives the free and spontaneous activity of the $νοῦς$, the mould or the raw material of creation. Thus after Timaeus invokes the gods anew, he remarks: 'This new beginning of our discussion requires a fuller division than the former.' Notice that all he claims to do here is not to *add a new nature of being*, a new genus overlooked in the previous

[13] On the meaning of the 'Spurious reason' see Zeller's *Plato and the Older Academy*, VII, note 60.

discussion, but simply to give a fuller division. For the genus of Becoming, before assumed to be simple, since the situation did not demand any further analysis, is now to be divided into its constituents for the purpose of bringing out the principle of ἀνάγκη in the universe. Heraclitus declared πάντα ῥεῖ, and Plato subscribes to that doctrine. Yet it needs some modification. True that the shape of the gold moulded by the goldsmith is mutable and transitory, yet behind there is abiding gold that one can point his finger to and say τοῦτο. Hence a thing of Becoming is not after all unique and simple, but behind the fleeting forms there is a more abiding substrate. Becoming, then, can be further classified into the two incoordinate elements, form and matter, and the latter is the principle of necessity, the invisible receptacle and nurse of generation.

But here (p. 51) an epistemological problem presented itself before Plato, and he digresses for a little while. If we see only forms and phenomena, what right have we to think of things in themselves, of Ideas? And how do we know that our mental representations have their corresponding objects in reality? A similar question might be asked: How do we know the nature of the invisible raw material? But here the answer is simple—empirically, by means of our senses. Fleeting images must have their more abiding receptacle. But by what channel do we cognize Being, the Ideas that are not perceptible to our sense? This involves Plato's whole theory of knowledge. There are two different kinds of cognition—mind and true opinion, the former seeing things *a priori*, without the aid of the senses, and the latter knowing things *a posteriori*, by experience. In correspondence to these two ways of knowledge we have the realm of Being perceived by mind, and the realm of Becoming, including both forms and matter apprehended by true opinion, which knows both the image and the thing. But this twofold classification does not exhaust all human cognitions. It does not include that dream-like knowledge, that mysterious, inexplicable 'spurious reason' which apprehends of a home of all created things, eternal and indestructible. It might be omitted in the story of the creation, for it neither plays the creative part of Being, nor is it the plastic element of Becoming, but stands alone in its eternity as the home of all created things, nay, as the stage upon which the whole drama of creation is performed, and the stage never enters into the plot of the drama; yet it cannot be overlooked as an object of cognition in the epistomological discussion. Hence Plato introduces here a correspondence to our third mode of apprehension, a new genus, 'a third nature, which is space'. After a few remarks on the nature of space, Plato returns (p. 53) to the story of creation, and having discussed the material essence of things, the universal chaotic mass, he now proceeds to tell how Demiurgus produced order and arrangement in the world, and the discussion of the material cause gives way to the formal cause in the generation of the universe.

Thus our problem is solved. It was a misunderstanding that led people to believe that in the description of the receptacle and of space Plato referred to one and the same thing. We have shown that on the contrary Plato conceived them to be two distinct natures; the one partaking in creation, the other containing creation; the one empirically apprehended, and the other independent of all sensations. And all the arguments that the supporters of the materialistic view of space endeavoured to draw from Plato's discussion of the receptacle, the matter of generation, are based on a misunderstanding.

What then are we to gather from Plato's genuine discussion of space? It is not material, for all material things are created and empirically given, while (p. 28) space is eternal, and beyond all experience. We derive the notion of space not from contact with external reality, as the father of English empiricism claimed, but it is an innate idea of the mind, that all created things must be in space. Psychologically, this view bears a striking resemblance to the Kantian conception of space, but metaphysically the two are diametrically opposed to each other. Indeed, according to Plato, space is not a mere *ens rationis*, for being eternal it existed ever before the birth of the human mind.

When we come down from Plato to his illustrious disciple, Aristotle, we feel somewhat relieved. To be sure the matter becomes more profound, the treatment more analytic, and we have now before us a procession of brilliant syllogisms, but the most profound syllogism may sometimes be more easily digestible by the human mind than the smallest figure of speech.

Aristotle's Conception of Space

III. That place [13a] exists is evident from our most ordinary experiments. Watch a vessel through which water flows out and air comes in. There has been a thorough change in the contents of the vessel, yet something remained unchanged, the stereometric content, the place, the cubic inch or cubic foot which does not change whether it

---

[13a] It is to be noted at the outset that our usual distinction between 'place' and 'space' does not exist for Aristotle. They are both identical.

contains air or water or any other material. Thus place evidently exists. And it has not only mere existence, but also different qualitative determination, namely, upward and downward; fire tends upward, and earth downward (Aristotle's *Acht Bücher Physik*, Prantl, IV, ch. 1). But what is the essence of space? Here a multitude of difficulties present themselves. We all know, of course, that it is characterized by three dimensions. But in what category is place to be put? It cannot be matter, for in that case we could not have a body in space without violating the law of impenetrability, according to which two bodies cannot occupy the same place at the same time. For if a body could absorb another equal body, it might go on with this process of absorption to such an extent that a drop of water might absorb the whole sea (IV, 8). Place then cannot be material, for then it could not form the receptacle for any material thing. On the other hand, it cannot be incorporeal for it has magnitude. Or is it perhaps the limits or the superficies of any body? Resuming our original experiment with the vessel, we find that while the superficies of water make way for the superficies of air, and these in turn make way for some other superficies, what we call space does not change, hence space cannot mean superficies.

Thus we have seen that space is neither matter, nor form, i.e. the superficies of matter. Indeed, matter and form are internal in any given body, while by space we commonly understand an external receptacle. For the same reason we cannot maintain that space is the interval between the superficies of an object; for an object may be taken out of its place and restored to it, but one cannot remove an object from its interval. Moreover, the identification of space with the interval of a thing will lead us into many absurdities.

In the first place, if by space we understand the interval pervading the water or the air passing through the vessel, then every particle of the moving body will be surrounded by a space, and consequently there will be an infinite number of spaces.

Secondly, a moving body moves in *space*, but the body contains in itself a space in the form of an interval. Hence space will move in space, which is absurd.

Thirdly, when the vessel which contains an interval moves and occupies another interval, we will have a fusion of two intervals or spaces, which is likewise absurd.

But if space is neither matter nor form, nor the interval of a thing, there remains only one more alternative, and that is the adjacent boundary of the containing body. Man, we say, is in the world by virtue of his being on the earth, and on the earth because of the limited area which closely comprises him. Thus by space we must understand nothing else than that which contains, i.e. the vessel of any given thing. The place of the sailor is in the boat, the boat is in the river, and the river is in the river-bed. But Aristotle is anxious to make of space an ultimate being, and hence maintains that strictly speaking space is not the boat, nor the river, for these are movable, and a movable space would signify a space moving in space, which is absurd. True space then is immovable. It is the extreme limit of the heavenly sphere in which all things move, but it is not itself moved. Consequently only that is essentially in space which is contiguously contained in that extreme immovable boundary. All other things are only accidentally so by virtue of their being a part of that which is essentially in space, just as we say, reason is in man, though strictly speaking it is only in the mind of man.

So far we have been discussing space as filled by this or that object, as πλέον, but there are some who believe in the existence of a κενόν, of pure and empty space unoccupied by any material being, whether earth, water, or air, a mere void, an absolute vacuum. And they support their belief with the following arguments. Motion is possible only through a vacuum; for if a body could move through and penetrate another body, a sea, as we have seen before, might be absorbed in a drop of water. And how could any absorbent material soak into itself any liquid without exhibiting any voluminous increase, if not for the intervening voids? Aristotle repudiates the existence of any vacuum. Attacking the argument from motion, he maintains that motion is rendered possible, not necessarily through a vacuum, but also through an exchange of places with another body. Similarly when an absorbent body attracts a liquid, it may not be because of inherent voids, but because it dispels another body, namely, air. Furthermore, the fact is that vacuum, far from helping a moving body, far from forming the *sine qua non* of motion, makes indeed the phenomenon of a moving body impossible. Let us first analyse the kinds of motion. There is a motion of fire upward, or of earth downward, i.e. natural motion; and there is a motion of the ball that has been cast, i.e. violent motion. Both kinds of motion are impossible, according to Aristotle, in a void.

The upward tendency of fire is possible only through the difference in the conditions of the place in which it tends, from the conditions of place to which it tends, but a void cannot have these differences, inasmuch as it is the privation of any properties or conditions. Hence natural motion in a vacuum is an impossibility.

Violent motion is similarly impossible in a void. For the projected ball, according to Aristotle, moves on by the impulse of the air behind, which being lighter tends to move faster than the ball; but in a void there is no air to keep the ball in motion. Furthermore, the velocity of any given body depends on the density of the medium and the weight of the body. All other things being equal, the rarer the medium, the quicker the velocity; the less the density of a medium, the less the time that it will take a body to move over a given space. And since the density of a vacuum is zero, the time in which a body undertakes to pass over a given distance will likewise be zero; that is to say, a body will move in a vacuum in no time, which is absurd. A similar 'absurdity' is reached when we consider the other determinant in a moving body, namely, its weight. The weight of a body is its power to cut its way through a given medium, but inasmuch as a void is the absence of any medium, all bodies, whether light or heavy, would fall with the same velocity, and according to Aristotle this again is absurd. Consequently motion, in any of its forms, would be an utter impossibility in a vacuum.

Or consider the void in which a body is placed. When a body is immersed in any liquid, the latter will either be compressed or displaced and dispelled. But it is inconceivable how a void, sheer nothingness, can either be compressed or dispelled. Evidently then the void will absorb into itself the immersed body. Now every body possesses magnitude; and if the void is real, how will one magnitude absorb another one without violating the law of impenetrability. Consequently Aristotle concludes a void does not exist. It should, however, be remarked that the argument is not altogether sound. The hypothetical reality of the void is not consistently maintained in this argument. In the first part Aristotle argues that the void, even if real, cannot be compressed or dispelled, because materially it is mere nothingness, yet in the latter part he argues that if the void be real it would absorb the immersed body and thus violate the law of impenetrability; but if its reality is not meant to be material, we have no case here of absorption, or any one *body* penetrating another.

How then does Aristotle explain the phenomenon of compression and condensation which is very often adduced as an argument in favour of the vacuum theory? And what constitutes the differences between a rare and a thick body? Is it not that the rare has many more intervening voids which become stuffed with matter when the given body is undergoing a process of condensation? No, according to Aristotle, the difference between a rare and a thick body is not that the one consists of segregated tinier particles than the other; in other words, the difference is not quantitative, but purely qualitative. Matter is never broken up or discrete, it is continuous and unique; but there are two states of matter, the rare and the thick. And these two qualitative states are not mutually exclusive, but each one harbours the potentiality of the other. Thus condensation and rarefaction really fall into Aristotle's conception of motion, inasmuch as they are both processes of realization of latent potentialities.

Let us now formulate briefly Aristotle's main thesis in the problem of space. The term 'space' conveys to us three distinct ideas: either the magnitude of any given body, i.e. extension, or the receptacle of a given body, i.e. its place, or mere magnitude not filled with matter, i.e. a void. Now empirical space was not at all a problem for Aristotle. He combated the notion of space as the 'interval' (διάστημα) of a given thing, but the existence of the 'interval' he never called in question. The Cartesian breach between mind and body, which led to the famous Kantian doctrine of the subjectivity of space, was yet unknown. The reality of any concrete magnitude is not called in question. As to the notion of place, according to Aristotle, it is nothing else than the relation of contiguity subsisting between two bodies. It does not represent, then, any entity of its own, whether material or spiritual. It is a relation, it is the point of contact between two concrete objects. Finally, as to the void, this is entirely non-existent, for the reason that since place is simply the relation of proximity subsisting between two things, there is no room left for mere extension outside of any concrete object or void. Hence space is finite, as finite as the material universe of which it is an expression of contiguous relationship.

It should, however, be observed that Aristotle was not consistent in this notion of place. He argues that place is essentially stable and immovable, for if it were movable it would move in place, *ergo*, place would be in place, which is absurd. Hence, only the all-containing diurnal sphere immovable—though revolving around its own axis—can be designated as essential place; otherwise we have only accidental place. Now imagine I have a coin in my hand, and I move my hand from point A to point B on my desk. To be sure, the place of my hand, that is to say, the relation of proximity between my hand and the point A changes, but the relation between the coin and my hand does not change. You may imagine also that while I move my hand from A to B the coin undergoes on its own account a simultaneous change of place-relation; but the two changes in place-relation are mutually independent, since point A is not the place of the coin. It is meaningless therefore to speak of space moving in space, if by the latter is meant merely a relation of contiguity. Thus Aristotle's distinction between accidental and essential place is unwarranted. Altogether one may speak of an object as being in motion, in the sense that the one and the same object preserving its whole identity changes its environment; but if by place we understand just this relation of environment it cannot strictly speaking move, for its whole identity is changed, and there is not one relation moving, but there are as many distinct relations as points of motion. It is the failure to realize this distinction between a relation and a thing, i.e. between place as relation and place as objective space, that makes the whole argument fallacious.

Thus I have presented before the reader two distinct views of space, the Platonic and the Aristotelian. The first, as I understand it, looks at the material universe as a small island in the midst of a vast infinite sea which we call space. The other takes no cognizance of imperceptible space, but apprehends only corporeal things and their relations. How far Jewish speculation was influenced by these two views, the subsequent pages will attempt to describe.

CHAPTER I

Empirical Space

I. That extensity is an indispensable element in our notion of matter was never questioned by Jewish thinkers. Yet the complementary idea that unextendedness is an indispensable element in our notion of spirit was less fortunate. The line of demarcation between matter and spirit was not distinctly drawn by some earlier Jewish thinkers. Subconsciously, however, they felt that an absolute spirit cannot be conceived in terms of magnitude. Hence, while the soul is sometimes spoken of in words that do not exclude extensity, it is always emphasized that the deity is beyond the category of space. Gradually the two types of reality were mutually divorced, and the principle soon acquired axiomatic certainty that unextendedness is the distinguishing mark of spirit, just as extendedness is the distinguishing mark of matter. Let us see how this change came about.

Beginning with Saadya of Fayum,[14] an author of the earlier part of the tenth century, we find that he accords to the soul only an intermediate position between matter and spirit. It is made of a luminous stuff that is finer than matter, though differing only in degree.[15] Hence the

[14] Saadya may be designated as the author of the first systematic presentation of the philosophy of Judaism, though by no means the pioneer in Jewish mediaeval speculation. Mention is to be made of Isaac Israeli of Kairwan, a thinker of note, who died one year before the completion of the *Emunot*, but whose philosophical fame was eclipsed by his fame as a physician. Cf. *Iggerot ha-Rambam*, p. 28, Leipzig, 1859.

[15] See *Emunot*, ed. Kitover. I have selected this uncritical edition for reference because of its being the most accessible. (A scholarly edition of the *Emunot* is now being prepared by Dr. Malter.) See also Horowitz, *Die Psychologie bei den jüdischen Religions-Philosophen*, I, 28.

problem of space and spirit did not present itself to Saadya in connexion with the soul. Perhaps his treatment of the deity, though belonging to the realm of theology, will give us a better occasion to learn what he thought of our problem. We find that Saadya lays special emphasis on the non-spatiality of God. By extensity, he says,[16] we mean two things, first the tridimensionality of an object, and secondly divisibility. An indivisible extensity is a contradiction of terms, for by extensity we mean a simultaneous continuity of parts. Feel this book, you have a sense of parts outside and alongside of each other, and you say it is extended. Thus our notion of the magnitude of an object is composed of the sense of its tridimensionality, and that of the 'alongsidedness' of parts or divisibility. But God cannot be said to be either tridimensional or divisible, hence he is beyond extension. In another place [17] he argues that only the material can be said to occupy space, which according to his conception means to come in contact with another body. When we say that an object moves in space we mean that there is always a point of contact, a *limit* between the earth and the body which encompasses it, namely, air, but we cannot perceive how the immaterial can meet a material body. Hence God is not in space. Saadya, it is to be noticed, alludes here to the Aristotelian conception of space, i.e. as 'the inner limit of the containing body', as we shall see in the sequel; but the basic idea of the argument is that inasmuch as by 'limit' we understand that point where a certain body ends and another body begins, and that alongside of that point there is a series of points which do not mark the beginning of another body; in other words, since a limit conveys to our mind a picture

[16] *Ibid.*, p. 96. [17] *Ibid.*, p. 99.

of a series, of a simultaneous succession of points, i. e. a picture of an *extended* object, the immaterial therefore cannot have any *limit*, for the spirit lacks the attribute of extension. Hence, when the prophets speak of 'God in heaven' they use metaphorical language, for surely they do not mean that God extends over, and is contained in the heaven.

But here we meet with a tremendous problem. How can we speak of divine omnipresence?[18] Omnipresence is the attribute of a thing which is here and there and everywhere, and that which has a 'here' and a 'there' has parts outside and alongside of each other, and is therefore extended, and to assume a divine omnipresence ought to be as non-sensical as to maintain a spiritual extensity or an extended spirituality. Saadya, however, is not ready to relinquish this fundamental dogma of religion. God, he explains, is present in the universe, as consciousness is in the body,

---

[18] See *Emunot*, p. 102. ואיך יעמד בשכלנו המצאו בכל מקום עד שלא יהיה מקום ריק ממנו? מפני שלא סר קודם כל מקום ואלו היו המקומות מפרידים בין חלקיו לא היה בורא אותם וכיון שהדבר כן המצאו אחר שברא הגשמים כולם כהמצאו קודם לכן בלא שינוי ולא פרידה ולא הסתר ולא הפסק. By the expression לא סר קודם כל מקום, Saadya does not mean that God existed spatially before creation, for that would be a flat contradiction to p. 99, where he says ועוד שלא סר לבדו ואפס מקום ואיננו נעתק בעבור בריאתו למקום, i.e. that God existed in no space before creation. There he also maintains that even after creation God must exist in no space, for else there would be a change in His being. Hence also the expression המצאו בכל מקום עד שלא יהיה מקום ריק ממנו cannot refer to any spatial existence. Evidently, then, Saadya means that while God is omnipresent, he is not at the same time extended; but he does not explain the apparent contradiction. An attempt at explanation he makes in the commentary on the Book of Creation, IV, 1, where he describes the deity as the consciousness of the universe, permeating the texture of the world by means of some rare and luminous gas. Comp. Kohler's *Grundriss einer systematischen Theologie des Judentums*, p. 73.

being found all in all and all in every part; and just as the soul maintains its material nature and indivisible integrity while being diffused over the body, so is God in the universe. Cut a limb off from a living body, and the soul is not lessened; annihilate a half of the universe, and the deity is not impaired. This explanation, however, can scarcely be designated a solution. It seeks to explain one difficulty by another difficulty, the difficulty of extended divinity by that of extended consciousness. Once you separate spirit from extension, you will find mind in space no more intelligible than God in space. Saadya, however, does not stand alone in the inability to cope with this tremendous problem. The human mind thinks in terms of the material data of human experience, it has no other data. Hence we are all labouring under a difficulty when we attempt not merely to *say* spirit but also to conceive spirit, whether mind or God. It is just as if the man born blind would attempt to conceive of colour. If, then, you accept the Cartesian dualistic position, you must end in sheer agnosticism of anything spiritual; or else, leaving God to the theologian, you must maintain that the human mind is not an entity *per se*, hiding itself in some recesses of our grey and white stuff—for the very fact that you speak of it as located in a certain place spatializes it—but that it is a mere quality of our brain-stuff, just as heat is the quality of a certain body, meaning by quality a certain state generated by changes in the relative position of the atoms. Similarly consciousness is a certain state generated by changes in the relative position of the neural atoms under the action of external stimuli. Thus following the Cartesian dualism to its logical conclusion we eventually land in material monism. But that seems to me the only safe position if we have no desire to entangle ourselves in the dilemma of space and spirit. But this is evidently too advanced for a mediaeval thinker, and I have permitted myself to digress in order to solicit our sympathy for Saadya and those who follow him in their vain attempt to solve a difficulty which still perplexes the human mind.

An advance in the conception of spirituality was made by Ibn Gabirol, who had the fortune of having his works quoted and discussed by the leading men of mediaeval scholasticism and his name forgotten.[19] He lays down a positive principle that anything simple and spiritual does not occupy space, and does not fall into the relation of near and far.[20] He goes beyond Saadya in considering the soul also an absolute *substantia simplex*, so that it is altogether beyond the category of space.[21] This uncompromising position opened before its author the wide chasm between mind and body. If the objective world is so essentially unlike the subjective world, what is it that transforms my impressions of external stimuli into a mental representation? And what is it that exchanges my purely mental act of volition into muscular activity? Gabirol attempts to bridge this chasm between soul and body. He finds in some sort of vital force (*spiritus*) a connecting link,

[19] *Orient. Lit.*, 1846, No. 46, and Munk's *Mélanges*, p. 152 ff.
[20] 'Omne simplex et spirituale locum non occupat.' *Fons Vitae*, p. 153. 'Substantia simplex non habet locum et omne quod non habet locum essentia eius aeque distat ab omni.' *Ibid.*, p. 156, on p. 120, he remarks: 'Substantia spiritualis non est terminabilis essentia quia non est quanta nec finita et quod fuerit terminabilis essentia eius essentia extenditur et est in omni loco'; but all he wishes to emphasize is, that of the spirit one cannot say it is here and not there. It has like relations in all spaces.
[21] 'Anima mobilis est per se non in loco,' p. 83. For the designation of the soul as *substantia simplex* see Horovitz's *Psychologie*, II, p. 108, note 65.

a 'causal nexus' between the two extreme forms of being.[22]
The problem, however, still remains; what is it that unites
this causal nexus to either mind and body?

After Gabirol, we find no Jewish philosopher questioning
the non-spatial nature of the soul. The problem now was
how to conceive of a non-spatial nature located in a certain
place. God is referred to very often both by Biblical
writers as well as by Talmudical sages as being in heaven.
Similarly the soul has been located by Aristotle in the
heart, and later by Galen in the brains. The opinion
has also been ascribed to Plato that every man harbours
in himself three souls, each one having its own habitation.
But how can a purely spiritual being be in a certain place?
When we say that the wine is in the flask, we mean that
there is a limit where the wine ends and the flask or the
walls of the flask begin. Strictly speaking, then, the

[22] See מקור חיים III, 3: והנפש נבדלת לגוף ולולי הרוח האמצעי
ביניהם לא היה דבק אחד מהם באחר. Compare the *Tractatus de Anima*
attributed by Munk to Gabirol, where we read: 'Simplex autem non potest
coniungi spisso sine medio quod habet similitudinem cum extremis. Item
anima non apprehendit sensibilia per se nisi mediante spiritu qui est substantia sentiens consimilis utrisque extremis et est media inter corporeitatem
sensibilium et spiritualitatem animae rationalis.' The notion of *ruaḥ* as
distinct from *nefesh* was very popular in mediaeval Hebrew literature. See
Steinschneider in *Hakarmel*, 1871, p. 400. See also *The Book of Definitions*,
by Isaac Israeli, the physician, published by H. Hirschfeld in Steinschneider's *Festschrift*, p. 138: ואם ישאלנו שואל מה פרק בין הנפש והרוח
נשיב להם כי הפרק ביניהם יהיה משתי פיאות כי הרוח הוא עצם גשמי
שמקיפו הגוף ואוחזו ומחזיק בו והנפש היא עצם רוחני שמקפת לגוף מחוץ
ומחזיק בו. Joseph ibn Aknin seems to have been conscious of these words
of Israeli when he wrote: הרוח גשם והנפש אינה גשם אלא צורה הרוח
מהלכת בשבילי הגוף והנפש לא יכילה הגשם. See his *Ethics*, p. 174
(*Sepher Mussar*, ed. Bacher, Berlin, 1910). Comp. also *Cosari*, p. 96:
והנפש לא תתחבר כי אם ברוח חם טבעי אי אפשר לו בלתי מקור שיקשר
לו כהקשר הלהב בראש הפתילה דמיון הפתילה היא הלהב.

'inness' of a thing implies a certain limit; but a limit is always the end of a series of points that are not limits; in other words, the end of a certain magnitude. But God and the soul are now conceived to be non-magnitudinal; how can we designate them as *in* a certain place? Surprisingly enough, the very author of the dualism of consciousness and extension, René Descartes, was guilty of the same fallacy. He located the soul in the pineal gland. We already saw Saadya finding difficulty in this idea. Judah Halevi explains it as follows: When we speak of God dwelling in heaven, we mean nothing else than that there the workings of the deity are most clearly and directly manifested; for below the heavens it works through natural agencies, and thus the divine plan can be discerned only indirectly. This explanation, it should be noted, is based on the pre-Newtonian distinction between the *natural* sublunary world and the *divine* superlunary world. Later Jewish philosophers differed in explaining the expression of 'God in heaven', but they all agree that it is not to be taken literally.[23] A similar explanation Judah Halevi offers for designating the soul as being in the heart, because the latter is the most vital organ, the centre of all blood vessels and arteries, and here again we do not mean exactly that the soul is physically situated in the heart.[24] The possibility of any place-relation between soul and body was further reduced *ad absurdum* by a younger contemporary of Halevi, namely, Joseph ibn Zaddik. In his little work entitled *Microcosm*[25] he argues: The soul cannot be in the body, for anything that is in another object is

---

[23] See Schechter, *Aspects of Rabbinic Theology*, p. 28 *et seq.*
[24] See *Cosari*, ed. Zefrinowitch, Warsaw, 1911.
[25] See *Microcosm*, ed. Horovitz, pp. 33, 36.

corporeal. Moreover, if it were in the body it would either be centralized in one particular place, or else extended all over the body; but in the first case the other parts will be soulless and dead, and in the other case a limb cut off would be so much of the soul taken away, which contradicts our conception of the integrity and indivisibility of the soul. But perhaps it is outside of the body?[26] Then we would have three alternatives: either the soul is removed from the body, or close to the body on one side, or else enveloping the body like a veil. Now the first alternative is impossible, for how would the body live when not in contact with the soul. The second alternative is impossible, for then the other side not touched by the soul would be lifeless; and the third one is equally impossible, for if it embraces an extended body it must itself be extended. It must have a certain magnitude; a pin-point cannot embrace a material object. But the soul is pure spirit, and altogether unextended. Hence any conceivable place-relation between soul and body is absurd. And yet we speak of a soul animating the body; consequently there must be some inter-relation between them. How is that relation to be understood? The answer to this question Joseph ibn Zaddik puts in very vague and ambiguous terms.[27] He speaks of

[26] Such a view indeed has been maintained as early as Isaac Israeli of Kairwan in the above cited passage from *The Book of Definitions*: והנפש היא עצם רחני שמקפת לנוף מחוץ ומחזיק בו.

[27] והנה התבאר ממה שהקדמנו שאינה לא גוף, עולם קטן, p. 36: ולא בגוף ולא חוצה לגוף אלא היא דקה מאוד והקפתה לגוף יותר דק מהקפת הגוף עצמו ויותר קרובה לגוף מקורבת חלק הגוף לגוף... הואיל ואינה בו כמו שבארנו שאין מקומה הגוף אבל הנפש מקום לו אבל מקום שכלי. Comp. p. 31: ולא יעלה על הדעת שזה הדיבוק שאמרנו בנפש. It is החכמה ובנפש החיה שהוא דיבוק נשמי אבל הוא דיבוק רוחני. strange that the vegetative soul is here altogether omitted, although on p. 37

the soul being finer than the mere extremities of the body, and adhering to it closer than one part of that body adheres to another. But all this should be taken as a strong effort to describe the spiritual nature of the soul in the terms of matter. And he warns us not to conceive of the interaction between mind and body as in any way material. It is a spiritual interaction.

Undoubtedly the reader will still be dissatisfied. A spiritual mode of interaction will suit the spiritual agent, but not the material recipient. The 'causal nexus' that Gabirol and Halevi found in the vital force is no longer applicable here. According to Joseph ibn Zaddik, the vital force itself is absolute spirit beyond the category of space,[28] he speaks of all the three souls as independent spiritual substances; and on p. 29 he maintains that, strictly speaking, it is just as improper to locate the vegetative soul in the liver as the vital soul in the heart, for location would imply spatiality, and hence corporeality. This omission is not merely incidental; it agrees with another passage on p. 28, where the reasons why the vital soul cannot unite with the body unless the latter has been already penetrated by the vegetative soul, is explained as follows: 'Body is dead, and the vital soul is the source of life; the first is fine and the latter is thick and earthly. Hence the body can unite with the soul only when already filled with the vegetative soul.' But the question suggests itself quite readily: How does the vegetative soul unite with the dead and coarse body? And if Ibn Zaddik meant to imply that the vegetative soul can come in contact with the body because it is near the material order of existence, how is it to be reconciled with the other statement that all three souls are spiritual and non-spatial? The contradiction is patent, and all we can do in this connexion is just to point to it, but not to remove it.

[28] Ibn Zaddik does speak of a רוח החיה, a vital force, but in his psychological system it is only one of the constituent forces of the vital soul, and is therefore pure spirit. Comp. on p. 28: ועל כן הנפש החיה היא נשואה ברוח החיה שהיא כח מכחותיה והרוח הזה החי נשוא בדם הזך אשר בעורקים. The term נשואה, however, is difficult, suggesting as it does that the רוח החיה is something independent of the נפש היה, which is expressly repudiated immediately by what follows. This vital force seems to

or any other material accessories. It is itself an extreme that needs a connecting link to come in touch with body. We welcome his elimination of the 'causal nexus' theory, which does not help the situation at all, and is fraught with logical difficulties, but on the other hand the doctrine of direct spiritual interaction leaves the problem still open on the side of the material recipient. However, occasionalism and parallelism, or any other doctrine invented for the purpose of justifying the dualistic standpoint, does not offer a more satisfactory explanation.

The dualistic position received its clearest formulation in the *Microcosm* of Joseph ibn Zaddik. It underwent no modification or further development in the systems of the Jewish philosophers that the Middle Ages produced after him. We are ready then to formulate our first thesis: Absolute spirit is distinguished from absolute matter in that it is altogether beyond all notions of spatiality. I say 'absolute spirit' and 'absolute matter', in order to include the first mediaeval thinkers, who though they entertained spatial notions regarding the soul, which was viewed as a somewhat material essence, yet removed all magnitudinal determinations from a truly spiritual essence, e.g. God. And if we consider that they lived in an age which was quite productive of queer mystic treatises on different ways of measurement of the deity and its various limbs, we will be in a position to realize the whole significance of the doctrine not only for the history of theology, but also for

---

be a superfluous appendix to his psychology, perhaps under the influence of Ibn Gabirol, though in his own system it is altogether meaningless. Comp. p. 28: הנפש החיה היא בלב נשואה בדם הנקי המתולעי אשר בלב, and on p. 29: שכחות הנפש החיה נשואים בדם אשר בלב, where this vital force is altogether omitted.

that of pure philosophic speculation. At first there was only the antithesis of God and corporeality, with mind occupying the middle ground, but the domain of spirit gradually appropriated all our psychic powers until the middle of the eleventh century, when strict dualism became the standard view-point in Jewish philosophy, a dualism of mind and body, the latter being extended in space and the former spaceless.

II. In the preceding discussion we have reached the conclusion that spatiality is the distinguishing characteristic of the corporeal world. Indeed, if you examine the different systems in Jewish philosophy you will find that they all concur in defining matter as that which has three dimensions. But this definition raises a very important problem, to which we will now direct our attention. Tridimensionality, we all agree, is the distinctive feature of matter, but does it constitute the very essence of matter? Evidently not: we can conceive of tridimensionality devoid of any material object. You may apply the air pump to your jar and thus remove the air almost completely, but you cannot remove the spatiality which still remains in the jar in spite of your efforts. Obviously the space does not constitute corporeality. And if we cannot say that a body is space, but that a body has space, the question remains what is body? What is it that hides itself behind a veil of tridimensionality?

Before we start our discussion of the Jewish view, however, let us attempt to examine the problem somewhat more closely, and get at the real issue. Pragmatically, it is to be noted, the whole question is meaningless. Reality consists of groups of sense-impressions which we call things, and with which we are constantly in relation and interaction; as for things-in-themselves, we have as little to do with them as with the Man-in-the-moon. When the food is tasty we are satisfied, but whether the food *per se* is tasty or not, we never seem to worry. Or, to take a nobler illustration, we rejoice on a bright summer day over a vast green lawn, but we are little concerned with the possibility of there being something that is neither vast nor green nor lawn. The pragmatist then may very well shrug his shoulders at the quibbling whether extensity is only phenomenal or also noumenal. Yet from the standpoint of the historical investigator, who is anxious to trace the links in the development of human speculation, even this quibbling becomes highly interesting. The problem is as follows: Every object presents itself to our minds in a variety of ways. The apple is perceived in the form of greenness of colour, roundness of shape, smoothness of touch, and sweetness of taste. Now some of these forms of perception, like colour and touch and taste, are undoubtedly subjective. The apple in itself unperceived by the human mind is devoid of these secondary qualities. We all admire the beauty of the rainbow, but in fact this beautiful array of colours is a creation of our visual apparatus; what we really have before us is a mere variety of absolutely colourless vibrations of ether. And now the question is: What of space? Is it also a sense-illusion, or is it real?

In the history of general philosophy we find that Aristotle understood his master to identify space with matter.[29] Whether it was a true understanding of Plato

---

[29] See *Phys.*, IV, 2 διὸ καὶ Πλάτων τὴν ὕλην καὶ τὴν χώραν ταὐτό φησιν εἶναι ἐν τῷ Τιμαίῳ... Ὅμως τὸν τόπον καὶ τὴν χώραν τὸ αὐτὸ ἀπεφήνατο. See *Tim.* 52 a. Comp. Baeumker, *Das Problem der Materie in der griechischen Philosophie*, pp. 177 ff.

or a misunderstanding, I have attempted to decide in the introduction. But mediaeval thinkers after all followed Aristotle, and were consequently influenced by this ascribed Platonic notion. A similar theory was maintained by Descartes, who in his zeal to widen the gulf between mind and matter, made extension the essential nature of things, and was consequently led to deny the existence of a void, for a void is abstracted spatiality, immaterial extension, which is from the Cartesian standpoint an absurd contradiction. We may mentally abstract, he argued, all characteristics by means of which the external world makes itself known to our senses, but we cannot abstract the element of spatiality without destroying our cognition. We may conceive of a colourless, tasteless, and odourless object, but we cannot conceive it non-extended. Hence extension must be the essences of an object, the primary quality, unbegotten by the mind and independent of all perception. The avalanche is none the less big in far off arctic regions where there is no human eye to perceive its 'bigness'. Space is that attribute of things without which their existence is utterly impossible.[30]

The same argument that led Descartes to maintain the absolute and unconditioned reality of space, induced Kant to uphold the ideality of space. If I cannot abstract the space element without destroying my cognition it does not follow that space is an external reality, for that will not account for the impossibility of a mental abstraction of spatiality, but it does follow that space is the mental condition and the indispensable framework for all perception. Just as when we look through blue spectacles,

---

[30] See Descartes, *Principes*, I, 63-4 ; II, 11.

we see a world of blue, blue suns and mountains and trees, so the mind, when it turns its gaze on the external world, puts on spectacles of spatiality and thus beholds a strange extended universe. Consequently things-in-themselves, independently of our senses, are beyond the category of space; it is the mind only that envelops them in a garb of extension ere it admits them into its own domain.

Thus we have three solutions to the problem of space and matter, each solution marking a certain state of progress in the development of human thought. First, we have the pseudo-Platonic theory which maintains that space is the undifferentiated material substrate of all things, the raw material which the architect moulded into the infinite variety of things, the wax upon which the great Demiurgus impressed his signet. Secondly, we have the Cartesian solution, according to which space is not matter, and the very ground-work of all things, but the primary distinguishing attribute of corporeality, meaning by 'primary' the only quality which really adheres to an external object independently of human perception, and by 'distinguishing' the only quality without which the existence of corporeality is unimaginable. Finally, we have the Kantian solution, according to which space is neither matter nor an unconditional attribute of matter, but a subjective form of intuition, a framework of sensibility.

Now what solution did the Jewish thinkers offer to our problem? It should be noted that virtually all of them define matter as that which has three dimensions, some even make tridimensionality itself the definition of matter, yet one must be cautious in drawing from this, usually careless, definition any conclusion regarding the reality of space. However, some Jewish thinkers were more explicit on that point. In his *Emunot we-Deot*[31] Saadya illustrates how one can rise from reflection on the empirical data of consciousness to the highest limit of human understanding, by first abstracting from any perceived body all the transient qualities like colour, heat, etc., then also abstracting the notions of extensity, and proceeding with this method of abstraction until the mind steps on the threshold of pure substantiality—Kant would have said the noumenon—which is beyond all human cognition. It is evident then that Saadya considers spatiality as something external to the essence of substantiality, as something that can be abstracted without destroying the concept, as something purely accidental. This view of space is strictly Aristotelian, in which system spatiality is one of the accidental categories of substance; and it is also shared by the Arabian school of thinkers going under the name of Brothers of Purity.[32] In Jewish circles it was by no means the predominant one, yet it found its adherents in Saadya, as already noted, in the staunch Aristotelian Moses Maimuni, and in a number of other thinkers. Maimonides especially maintained that spatiality does not constitute substantiality, that a substance consists primarily of matter and form, both of them indescribable in terms of extension which is only accidentally attached to them.[33] Similarly, Samuel ibn Tibbon holds that magnitude is an accident only, that substance is conceivable without it.[34] Indirectly,

---

[31] See *Emunot*, p. 84.

[32] Dieterici, *Naturanschauung*, p. 29: 'Der Raum ist eine von den Eigenschaften der Körper, er ist ein Accidens, das nur am Körper besteht und nur an ihm sich findet.'

[33] *Guide*, I, 76.

[34] Scheyer in *Das psychologische System des Maimonides* (Frankfurt a. Main, 1845, p. 110) thinks that Ibn Tibbon opposes Maimonides in this regard, and

from a pupil of the famous astronomer of the University of Padua, Elijah del Medigo, we learn that the latter held the same view.[35] Abrabanel[36] and R. Jehiel b. Samuel of Pisa,[37] both authors of the sixteenth century, also subscribe to that theory of space, according to which it does not play an essential rôle in our conception of pure matter. Thus, one view of the reality of space is the Aristotelian one. Extension does not enter our notion of corporeality, though no one assumed the existence of unextended matter. Snow is always white, yet whiteness is by no means the essence of snow; so matter is always extended, yet extensity is not the essence of matter. It is an inseparable accident.

Over against this view we have one that is more akin to the pseudo-Platonic conception. It was first voiced very emphatically by an older contemporary of Saadya, Isaac

he cites as proof the fact that the former defined matter as that which has three dimensions ונדר הגשם הוא כל דבר שיש לו שלשה רחקים והם אורך רוחב וגבה (רוח חן פ״א). But this definition, far from bearing witness to a substantialistic theory of space, might suggest the opposite, for it includes in the make-up of matter something that *has* tridimensionality and hence beyond it. This latter view is indeed explicitly maintained by Ibn Tibbon in the tenth chapter of the same work, where we read: ואין ספק כי הכמות הוא מקרה לעצם הנושא כי האורך והרוחב והגבה וכן האחדות והשניות והשלשיות אינם עצם הדבר ואין משלימים אמתת העצם ההיא אם כן היא דבר אחר מקרי לעצם. But this passage was altogether overlooked by Scheyer, and also by Schmiedel, who followed him blindly. (See his *Studien über Religionsphilosophie*, Wien, 1869, p. 277, n. 2.) It is also noteworthy that it is by no means certain that Samuel Ibn Tibbon is the author of the pamphlet entitled *Ruaḥ Hen*. But the other theories are no less probable. At any rate it is the work, not the authorship, that is important in this connexion.

[35] See שאלות שאול הכהן, p. 10.
[36] *Ibid.*, p. 20.
[37] See *Minḥat Kenaot*, ed. Kaufmann (Berlin, 1898), p. 37.

Israeli, in his statement that 'tridimensionality is matter, and matter tridimensionality'.[38] Israeli seems to have held this doctrine, a truism, an axiom of thought which requires no proof. Later thinkers were somewhat less confident in this regard. Yet the conclusions of some of them at least were not substantially different. Gabirol considers all existence, both material and spiritual, essentially one. The divine intellect and the mute rock are, according to him, made up of the same matter; it is only the form, the differentiating principle in the universe, that made one mute and the other mental. The genesis of the Universe was then as follows: Originally there was the *hyle*. Then the *hyle* was divided in two, one part of which assumed the form of spirituality, and the other corporeality. Then each great division further divided itself, and again subdivided itself, giving rise to the infinite variety of things, each step in this great evolution being a form to that which preceded and matter to that which is to follow. If we take a flower, we may trace back the different stages that this flower stuff underwent on its march from the *hyle*. Let us consider the few more conspicuous stages.[39] Our first impression of the flower is the red colour, and we call it the quality-form. But redness has no existence *per se*. What is it that is red? You will say, of course, the flower is red. But the flower nature is present in each one of its minute particles, yet each minute particle is not red, just as each thin leaf of a gilt-edged book is not perceptibly gilt;

---

[38] See *Sefer Yesodot*, ed. Fried, Drohobycz, 1900, p. 47.

[39] Cf. *Fons Vitae*, p. 204: ' Et quo magis redierit et exierit a *substantia ad quantitatem* et a quantitate ad *figuram* et a figura ad *colorem*, manifestius fiet ei esse propter crassitudinem suam.' Notice the four stages in the genesis of all things: (1) substance, by which is meant the first matter; (2) quantity; (3) shape; (4) colour.

consequently a flower is red only by means of extensity, which stands in the same relation to colour as matter is to form. Now analyse further and inquire what is extensity, and what is it that sustains it. Gabirol's relativism prevents him from halting at extensity, though he identifies it with corporeality; and hence he maintains that extensity is the form which combines with the original undefined hylic matter. And even before subjecting itself to the categories of accident, the substance that the Greeks called $\mu\epsilon\tau\alpha\xi\acute{\upsilon}$,[40] i.e. the first compound of matter and form was already extended. Thus Gabirol's view on our problem is clear, though expressed in the very vague and disputed terms of matter and form. Extensity is not a phenomenon of corporeality like colour, sound, smell, but that of which they are phenomena, that is to say, corporeality itself.[41]

[40] Whether Aristotle assumed a *metaxu* was one of the issues in the Neumark-Husik controversy, for which see *Archiv für Geschichte der Philosophie*, XXIII, 4, 1910, and XXIV, 3, 1911. It is curious, however, that Isaac Abrabanel seems to have foreseen this controversy, and decided the case in favour of Husik, see שאלות שאול הכהן, p. 20. Yet one is no heretic if he doubts Abrabanel's authority for Aristotle.

[41] *Fons Vitae*, p. 229: 'Sed vides quod *materia corporalis*, i. e. *quantitas* quae sustinet formam coloris et figurae non est forma corpori quod eam sustinet sicut qualitas, i.e. color et figura est forma illi.' Cf. also Guttmann's *Die Philosophie des Solomon Ibn Gabirol*, p. 180. On p. 293, Gabirol remarks: 'Oportet ut scias quod qualitas etsi adiacet quantitas, hoc non est nisi quantum ad sensum sed certe quantitas et qualitas simul sunt, ideo quod color et figura comitantur corpus universaliter.' Gabirol does not mean to imply that the essential nature of extension is a mere sense-illusion; but that though colour is accident and quantity substance, still both are equally necessary for the perfection of matter. The expression *comitantur corpus* is somewhat misleading, but its meaning becomes evident on comparing the Hebrew Text of Palquera which reads אבל על האמתה הוא והכמות יחדיו כי הגון והתבנית מתחייבים לכלות (i.e. to perfect) הגשם (מקור חיים, 24). Schmiedel (*l. c.*) here, again, overlooked all these passages and cites only the passage in *Meḳor Ḥayyim*, II, 2 : (i.e. a body) וכשתגדור אותו תאמר שהוא

Gabirol, it is true, posits in every corporeal object an unextended hylic element, and in this respect he dissents from the pseudo-Platonic view which considers space itself the hylic element; but the *hyle* as used by Plato denotes a greater reality—if the latter can at all be said to be greater or smaller—than the *hyle* of Aristotle and the mediaeval thinkers, so that the two views are at bottom one. For our discussion we may eliminate altogether the mysterious *hyle* which tends to confuse the whole argument, and thus formulate Gabirol's position as follows: Extendedness is the essence of a thing or the thinghood; all other notions we have of an object are unimportant accident. The mathematician, Abraham b. Hiyya, adopted a similar view, and defined matter as tridimensionality plus something, the first term being the form of corporeality, and the second the indeterminate *hyle*.[42]

The same attitude was taken by the author of the *Microcosm*, Joseph Ibn Zaddik.[43] Tridimensionality, he

הארך והרחב והעמק, and tries to find the cause of the disagreement between Gabirol and Maimonides as to the reality of space in their different attitudes on a certain point in the problem of matter and form, but he misses the real problem at issue. Comp. also Scheyer's *Psychologisches System des Maimonides*, p. 110.

[42] See חובות הלבבות, p. 2.

[43] His meaning is at first glance not very clear and consistent. On p. 7 of the *Microcosm* Joseph Ibn Zaddik says: החומר הראשון אשר לבש צורת הגשמות ונעשה עצם גשמי ולא השיגו ממקרה הגשמות אלא שהוא ממלא מקום והראיה שכל חומר מאליו מובדל מן האחר הוא שכל אחד ממלא מקומו יחלק חבירו בקלות וכבידות ובקור ובחום. Thus he thinks that 'filling space' is an accident. Now turn to p. 9: ובלבשו הצורה הגשמית נעשה בגללו הגוף מורכב לפי שקבל היסוד הארוך והרחב והעומק שאלה הם צורת הגשמות וכשרדבקו בו הגבולים השלשה הנזכרים האלו מלא מקום ובהיותו ממלא מקום קבל שאר המקרים הגשמיים המושגים בהרגש. Here he holds that tridimensionality is the form of matter, while

asserts, is the form and essence of corporeality, which the *hyle* assumes in the process of actualization; yet impenetrability he maintains is a mere accident. An accident is an unessential element in the conception of a thing, and we can very well conceive of a substance as pure extensity without thinking of that property by virtue of which it resists any body attempting to take its place. In fact, geometrical bodies are not impenetrable; a thousand angles may occupy the same space. And this author evidently applies the conception of ideal matter to real matter. It is the geometrician who deals with the ultimate essence of things, all other scientists with mere accidents.

A slightly divergent view was maintained by Abraham Ibn Daud in his work entitled *The Exalted Faith*. This author points out that tridimensionality is not the essence of matter, but an accident. Quantity is one of the nine accidental categories. It is accidental because it is not permanent and immutable. From the same piece of wax— let us say ten cubic cm. in volume—you can mould any number of objects with an infinite variety of dimensions. 'filling space' is accident. Similarly, on p. 13, where he remarks: כי היסוד הנושא לארבע הטבעים האלו הוא עצם מחזיק מקום בלבשו צורת הגשמות שהוא האורך והרחב והעמק וכשימלא מקום יתנועע. When we examine, however, the meaning of the expression 'filling space' in the first quotation, we are led to suspect that it corresponds to the idea of impenetrability. This is corroborated by a study of this term as used by other authors. It is similar to the expression יטריד מקום 'occupying space'—both corresponding to the Arabic يشغل مكان, sometimes used to convey the sense of impenetrability. Comp. Crescas, *Light of God*, p. 14: שהרחקים בעלי חומר יטרידו המקום אשר מזה הצד הוא נמנע הכנס גשם בגשם. Compare also the *Microcosm* itself, p. 15: דע כי ענין הגוף שהוא ממלא מקומו וכל זמן שמקומו מלא ממנו לא יתכן לגוף אחר להגיע לאותו מקום. The author's view then is clear. Extensity is the ultimate nature of matter; impenetrability is a mere accident. See Appendix, s. v. מקום.

You may say that though each one of these moulded objects has different dimensions, yet they all have the same amount of voluminousness, i.e. ten cubic cm. But melt this piece of wax and you get a different quantity altogether. Hence, when the geometrician comes to represent the ultimate essence of this piece of wax and draws a figure ten cubic cm. in volume, he is wrong, because the quantity changes, while our notion of substantiality implies an immutable and indestructible nature. But if the latter is not to be found in the specific amount of extensity, it is to be found in the *abstract* notion of extensity.[44] When a gas is condensed into a liquid, and that in turn into a solid, the quantity of extensity varies of course, yet they are all extended in the same degree. And the essence of matter is extensity. But does not the compressed liquid have less of extensity than the free gas? Yes, but extensity as the ultimate nature of things is not to be viewed quantitatively, but qualitatively. It is the quality of matter to be extended just as it is the quality of man to live. And from this standpoint a blade of grass and a vast landscape exhibit the same degree of the *quality* of spatiality. It is this indivisible spatiality which forms the essence of matter, and any question of more and less confuses the argument by introducing a foreign element, i.e. quantitative spatiality.

This view of Abraham Ibn Daud was adopted by the famous disciple of Maimonides, Joseph Ibn Aknin.[45] And

[44] See *Emunah Ramah*, I, 1, 2.

[45] See Moritz Löwy, *Drei Abhandlungen*, pp. 12, 13: שהנגשם מליצה מהדבקות אשר אפשר שיונחו בו שלשה שלוחים כריתותם על זויות נצבות ואחד השלוחים יקרא אורך והאחד רוחב והשלישי עמק ר"ל גובה וזה הוא ענין הגשמות הנמצא בהיולי ראשונה בלתי בחינת צורה אחרת ואינה נפש.
(And here one codex has the following insertion: ר"ל כי השלשה שלוחים

it is strange that Don Isaac Abrabanel [46] ascribes this view to Ibn Aknin, and gives no credit to Ibn Daud. Interesting are the two objections that Abrabanel quotes to this profound view—objections that do not evince a full grasp of Ibn Daud's theory. One objection is attributed to Averroes, and may be stated as follows: Extensity means continuity; and when a continuous object is broken up it loses its former continuity; hence extensity is itself transient, and presupposes another immutable essence which we might term substance. But this objection evidently loses sight of the distinction between quantitative and qualitative space: when a body is broken up, its quantitative extensity is lessened, but its qualitative extensity remains unchanged. Strangely enough, even Ibn Aknin, who follows Ibn Daud in his view on space and matter, apparently attempts to reconcile this view with Averroes's objection, and explains it thus: [47] True that extensity is the essence of matter, but it is only the formal essence; for

אינם עצמות הנשם מאשר הם בפועל כי יקבלו השווי התוספת והחסרון והצורה העצמית לא תומר ולא תתחלף א"כ הצורה היא הדביקות לבד לא . . השלוח כי השלוח מקרה ממאמר הכמה יומר ויוסיף ויהסר בחומר האחד . . . הנה הצורה אינה השלוח אבל הדביקות אשר יונח בה (השלוח והנשמים כולם משתתפים בצורת הדביקות).

[46] See שאלות שאול הכהן, p. 18: כי הנה כת אחת מהם חשבו כי הצורה הנשמות היא הדבקות ושהמרחקים הם מקרים בו ושמזה היה אבו אל חנאג יוסף יחייא הישראלי המערבי ונמשך אחריו אבו חמד ומפני זה גדר הנשם שהוא שאפשר שיונחו בו שלשה שלוחים נחתכים על זויות נצבות.

[47] Ibid.: ונבאר זה ונאמר שהנשם מליצה מהדבקות והדביקות אינו מקבל הפירוד והמקבל הוא אשר ישאר עם הקבלה והדביקות לא ישאר עם קבלת הפירוד אבל הפירוד יעדר ממנו והוא בלתי מקבלו הנה המקבל דבר בלתי הדביקות ועליו ישוב הפירוד והדביקות בבא זה אחר זה.

It is strange that Averroes is not mentioned.

since it is itself a variable, there must be an external hylic essence behind it. But there are two fallacies in this argument. First, if extensity changes, it cannot be form which is coeternal with the *hyle*; secondly, extensity qualitatively considered is unchanging, and there is no difficulty at all. The second objection, anonymously quoted, also misses the real point. How can we conceive of extensity without the notion of dimensions? Of course it is conceivable, just as life is conceivable as a *quality* without the notion of the *quantity* of its duration. Space as a quality is simple and indivisible, and this is the ultimate nature of matter; space as a quantity is composed and divisible. It can be augmented and lessened, and is a pure accident of matter.

It is to be regretted that this novel and profound view of space did not find more adherents in Jewish philosophy. Perhaps it was too advanced for the period. It was one of those sparks of truth flashing before their time, soon forgotten in the surrounding darkness. After Aknin, the view of Gabirol, Abraham bar Hiyya and Joseph Ibn Zaddik was resumed in its original vague form. Moses Narboni,[48] Shem Tob b. Shem Tob,[49] Abraham Bibago,[50] Aaron of Nicomedia, the Karaite,[51] all teach that space is the ultimate

---

[48] *Ibid.*, p. 9 b : אמר החכם הנרבוני כי ירצה הצורה הגשמיות אשר היא המרחקים המשולחים הבלתי מוגבלים בעצמם והיא הצורה האחרונה אשר היא בלתי הווה ולא נפסדת. It is not clear what he meant by 'indeterminate space' as form of matter, Abrabanel (*ibid.*, 19 a) rightly objects that form is actual, and everything real and actual is spatially determinate. Perhaps Narboni also had in mind the pure and qualitative extensity of Ibn Daud.

[49] *Ibid.*, p. 10 b.   [50] *Ibid.*

[51] See his work called *Eṣ Ḥayyim*, ed. Delitzsch, Leipzig, 1841, p. 43 : וידעת מה שיתבאר בס' המחקר כי הקו הוא אורך בלי רוחב ובלי עמק

form, the essence of corporeality. As no one of them added anything original to the conception, they may be dismissed without comment. The problem of space and the ultimate nature of matter did not cease to perplex the minds of thinkers, and as late as the sixteenth century we find a certain Rabbi Saul, a pupil of Elijah Delmedigo, still groping his way, unable to grasp how pure extensity can be the material essence of all things, turns to Don Isaac Abrabanel to lead him out of the tangle. Abrabanel analyses the various views and finally decides: Space is only an accident of things, an unessential element in the conception of matter.

Thus, to sum up, there are two rival views in Jewish philosophy as to the problem of the relation that space bears to matter, the Aristotelian and the pseudo-Platonic. Some uphold the first theory and maintain that space is not an essential nature, that we might conceive an unextended book or table, indeed the whole world of matter, in a pin-point. Others are shocked by this view. If there is any matter at all, it must be spatial. This is how the mind conceives of matter as distinguished from spirit. The one is a *res extensa*, the other a *res cogitans*. Thus while some of the adherents of the latter view, like Isaac Israeli of Kairwan and Aaron of Nicomedia the Karaite, go as far as

והשטח הוא הארך ורחב בלי עמק והגוף הוא אורך ורחב ועמק וא״כ על אלו הרחקים הוסכמה מלת גוף וכל העצמים בין היותם דומים בין היותם בלתי דומים ויהיו להם אלו הג׳ רחקים שהם ארך רוחב ועמק שם גוף אמרו לכולם בהסכמה. Compare an earlier Karaite of the middle of the twelfth century, Judah Hadassi, who in his *Eshkol Hakofer*, ch. 65, defines matter as that which has length, width, depth, and *thickness*: כל דבר שיש לו ארך רחב ועמק ועובי הוא יקרא גוף בלשונך, implying that tridimensionality needs yet another element, perhaps, hardness, in order to constitute matter. Aaron evidently disagrees.

imagining the world, stripped of its accidents, which are superfluous both logically and ontologically—the world in its essential and permanent nature, a network of fine lines like telegraph wires without the poles, the meshes corresponding to concrete objects; others do not take such a thoroughgoing geometrical view of reality, and assume the existence of some hylic nature filling the great vacuum, together constituting matter. This substantialistic view of space is further modified by Ibn Daud, who is followed by Ibn Aknin. Space is the essence of all things, not as quantity, for then it is a variable compound, and cannot be therefore ultimate reality, but the simple and indivisible quality to be extended, which is present in the same degree in the tiniest grain of sand and in the unmeasurable ocean.

III. In the preceding discussion the reader was undoubtedly impressed by the fact that while the pseudo-Platonic and the Aristotelian or Cartesian views found their representatives in Jewish philosophy, one seeks in vain for any traces of the Kantian doctrine on the subjectivity of space. This may be a source of disappointment or gratification, but it is not strange. The mediaeval thinkers were not yet so critical and distrustful with regard to their senses. Their theory of knowledge was absolute empiricism. Why should we doubt the existence of a thing which we may see and feel in various ways? Hence even those who upheld the view of the accidental nature of space, nevertheless agreed that it is a characteristic indispensable—at least in experience—of every material object. It was with them an axiom of unquestionable certainty that all existent things are extended.

But this leads us to another problem which played a very prominent rôle in the history of thought. Suppose we take a material object and divide it and subdivide it, and carry on this process of subdivision *ad infinitum*. Of course the extensity of the thing will shrink and shrivel, but in this process of subdivision are we ever going to reach a piece of matter so infinitely small as to be altogether unextended? Our first thought answers: Yes, every process must have an end. But this would contradict our previous conclusion that matter must have magnitude, unless of course we assume that in this infinite process of division matter together with space is annihilated—a very improbable assumption, because it questions the law of indestructibility of matter, which no mediaeval thinker would dare. Briefly, the problem of infinite divisibility of space, and hence also of matter, presents itself for our attention.

The doctrine of infinite divisibility is as ancient as Aristotle, and together with all other views of this matter, it held sway over human minds in the Middle Ages. But the Mutakallimun, the Arabian theologians whose influence on mediaeval thought was not insignificant either, held a different view on this matter. They were atomists. Apparently it is strange that a system which was founded by Democritus, and developed by modern scientists with no other motive than the removal of an intelligence, working behind the veil of phenomena, was advocated also by theologians who sought to bring the theological element of nature to the foreground. But really those Arabian scholastics were not inconsistent in this regard. The Greek and the modern atomists considered the atoms ultimate realities unbegotten and indestructible, whereas according to the Mutakallimun atoms perish, and new atoms are born at every moment. Along with the atomism of space there is an atomism of time. There is a continuous creation as well as a continuous destruction in the whole universe. An angel of death and an angel of life walk arm in arm in the infinite voids of space and time. There is nothing lasting two moments—is the favourite maxim of those thinkers. What then is it that abides in the midst of the universal and eternal change and decay? Nothing else than the Deity—answer the Mutakallimun triumphantly. Thus atomism is accorded a prominent place in the theological system of the Arabs.

I mentioned the atomic theory as disputing the field with the Aristotelian notion of infinite divisibility. The reader may not at first realize the dispute between the two theories. An explanatory word is necessary. Etymologically, 'atom' means indivisible. But the term 'indivisible' is ambiguous. The chemist seeks to know the elements that enter in the composition of a certain piece of matter and the proportion of their reaction, and when he gets at the unit of reaction, at that tiny being which is just big enough to unite with others and form this visible universe, he is satisfied. He has the atom; and indeed, chemically, it is no further reducible. The physicist, however, who is interested not only in its mode of reaction upon others but also in its own independent nature, finds that 'indivisible' is a misnomer. Minute as it may be, it has magnitude and part out of part, consequently it is a composite. Thus we see that the chemical notion of indivisibility does not conform to the physical notion. Now the Mutakallimun considered the atom indivisible in this last physical sense, while the Greek and the modern scientists use the chemical notion of indivisibility. The Moslem theologians think that matter is composed of ultimate particles indivisible and altogether spaceless by themselves, forming space by their combination. We see now wherein Arabian atomism opposes the Aristotelian doctrine of infinite divisibility. It maintains that if you will carry on your process of division long enough, you will eventually reach an atom indivisible, and filling no space at all, a mathematical point.

Did Jewish philosophy endorse the atomistic doctrine of the Kalam? Our answer is in the negative. Altogether the Kalam was not a prevalent doctrine among the Jewish thinkers, though it found adherents in Karaitic circles;[52] but Arabian atomism, as distinguished from the Greek and modern type, was mainly rejected. Abraham ibn Ezra[53] was the only Jewish thinker who favoured Arabian atomism; while, even among the Karaites, it found an early opponent in Judah Hadassi.[54] Thus Jewish philosophy may be said to be in opposition to the atomic theory, and in favour of the Aristotelian doctrine of infinite divisibility. Let us examine some of its arguments.

Already Isaac Israeli of Kairwan,[55] elder contemporary of Saadya, devotes considerable space to the atomistic doctrine of finite divisibility. He refers to Democritus whom he misunderstands. Democritus, according to Israeli, maintained that matter is composed of spaceless atoms,

---

[52] The Karaitic thinkers were generally inclined towards the Kalam. Indeed, they even assumed the name of Mutakallimun. See *Cosari*, VI, 5. The Rabbanites, however, were usually Aristotelians. Comp. *Guide*, ed. Munk, I, 339, note 1.

[53] See *Kerem Ḥemed*, IV, 2 and Appendix, s. v. מקום. On the authenticity of these fragments see Schreiner, *Der Kalam in der jüdischen Literatur*, p. 35.

[54] See *Eṣ Ḥayyim*, ch. 4. ואולם רבנו יהודה האבל נ״ע לא הסכים להיות הרכבת הגופים מן הדקים וכו׳. Comp. *Eshkol Hakofer*, p. 65.

[55] See his *Book of Elements*, ed. Fried (Drohobycz, 1900), p. 43.

or points. But the union of two points can be conceived in two ways: either the totality of the one unites with the totality of the other, or a part of the one comes in touch with that of the other. Now the first case leaves no separation or distance between the two points, and hence the result of the synthesis would be a point, and the second case involves the contradiction of a partial union of atoms that are by hypothesis spaceless and devoid of parts. For by a spaceless object we understand something which has no opposite sides: that point which indicates its beginning also indicates its end. Consequently mathematical points can never produce an extended object.[56] The underlying idea of the second part of the syllogism, namely, that any object that has two sides, has part out of part, and is therefore spatial, recurs in the works of the second Israeli[57] and of Aaron of Nicomedia.[58]

Saadya also combats vigorously the conception of mathematical points as the ultimate unities of extension. An indivisible atom, finer than any fine thing conceivable, almost a spiritual essence, is altogether unintelligible.[59] But he also realizes the tremendous difficulty connected with the theory of infinite divisibility. If a body can be divided *ad infinitum*, it must be composed of infinite particles. Infinite means endless, that is, there is no end to the particles in any given distance, great or small. There is a difficulty already, namely, that of a given finite line being infinite, for a line is the sum of its particles. Let us, however, overlook this ontological objection and ask a simpler question. We constantly see before us things

[56] This ingenious argument is drawn from Aristotle's *Physics*, VI, 1.
[57] *Yesod Olam*, I, 23.
[58] *Eṣ Ḥayyim*, p. 7.   [59] *Emunot*, p. 63.

moving, but how is motion possible? Imagine a given line AB having infinite particles, and a point P moving from A to B. Now it is absolutely immaterial

$$A \overset{P}{\rule{4cm}{0.4pt}} B$$

whether AB represents a mile or a yard or a fraction of an inch, it is infinitely divisible, and has infinite parts. And the point P must move over one part after another, one after another; and in order to land at B, it must have completed an infinite track, and reached the end of an endless series, which is impossible and absurd. It can also be shown that P cannot even commence to move, for the tiniest bit of the line is infinitely divisible, and P finds before itself an immeasurable abyss in order to reach the very next point. All of which goes to prove that motion is a mere illusion, or else the theory of infinite divisibility is false.[60]

The reader will have recognized the paradox of Zeno of Elea. The difficulty is truly tremendous to-day no less than twenty-five centuries ago. Saadya states that this objection led some thinkers to reject the theory of infinite divisibility—which means to face other difficulties; others—to assume that the moving point hastens some part of the way in order to make up for the infinite—which is the view of the Najimites; and, as Schahrastani remarks, hasty or slow, it must go through an infinite;[61] still others—to maintain that time is also infinitely divisible, each infinitesimal space corresponding to an infinitesimal time, and altogether P moving over a finite space in a finite time—an explanation which only intertwines one difficulty with another. Saadya's own explanation is as follows. The

[60] *Ibid.*, p. 59.   [61] See Schahrastani (Haarbrücker), I, 56.

theory of infinite divisibility claims by no means that there is actually unlimited division. The fact is that if we continue to break up a given particle long enough, we eventually reach a *minimum sensibile*, and there our process of division must end. By means of magnifying glasses and exceedingly fine instruments this *minimum sensibile* becomes a composite, and is further divisible; the limit of division is pushed a little further, but a limit there is after all. Thus there is no such thing as infinite divisibility as far as actual experience is concerned. All that is claimed is, that the *mind* conceives no limit to the possibility of dividing a given body, for this reason: that small as an object may appear to our senses, we may conceive of a microscope that magnifies the object a hundred-fold, and when the *minimum sensibile* is reached under this lens we may exchange it for another that has the power to magnify the object a thousandfold, and number is infinite. Consequently we can *mentally* divide an object *ad infinitum*; but only mentally, in reality we sooner or later get an ultimate empirically irreducible unit, a *minima pars*. Hence the possibility of motion which is a phenomenon of reality.[62]

The explanation is by no means clear and cogent. Chiefly there is this difficulty. We may fail to dissect an object experimentally into an infinite number of parts, but if our reason for maintaining the theory of infinite divisibility is valid—and Saadya claims that it is valid within its sphere—there are in that object an infinite number of points which, though empirically unknown, the moving body must pass over successively until the end of the endless series is reached, which is absurd. Thus Zeno's paradoxical ban on motion on the basis of the assumption

[62] See *Emunot*, p. 59, and compare *Cosari*, p. 183.

of infinite divisibility is scarcely removed. Saadya's view might suggest the existence of two kinds of space—one perceptual and real, the other conceptual and ideal; the former of a discrete nature, the latter continuous and infinitely divisible, so that both our perception and our reason are unerring within their distinct spheres; but it is highly improbable that Saadya would have taken such a dualistic standpoint. Briefly, then, Saadya introduced Zeno's paradox in Jewish philosophy, but could not explain it himself. This was left for a later thinker.

A strong plea for infinite divisibility is found in the second book of Gabirol's *Fons Vitae*. Extensity and indivisibility, he argues, are altogether two different kinds of being, the one is matter and the other spirit; and it is impossible to reduce one kind of being into an essentially different one. Hence the impossibility of matter being composed of indivisible and spaceless atoms, or, as Gabirol calls them, *minimae partes*.[63] It is not denied that there is a *minima pars* as far as our perception is concerned.[64] There is a *terminus a quo* to human vision. We cannot see very well a magnitude smaller than a hair's breadth. But the visual *limen* is not one for all men. It is relative only; a very keen eye may see things entirely hidden from the normal sight. Our perceptual *limen* does not at all empty

---

[63] *Fons Vitae*, p. 57 : 'Impossible est invenire partem quae non dividitur, eo quod omnes longitudines corporis sunt divisibles usque in infinitum et necesse fuit omnes longitudines corporis esse divisibiles usque infinitum ideo quod impossibile est aliquid resolvi in non genus suum si enim proposita pars quantitatis resolveretur in partem quae non dividebatur, necesse esset quod pars illa aut non esset aut esset substantia simplex.' Comp. Israeli's *Book of Elements*, pp. 43, 47 ff.

[64] 'Non est impossibile hanc partem esse minimam partium quantum ad sensum non in se.' *Ibid.*, p. 56.

the ontological existence of a *minima pars*. If mathematical points were the ultimate constituents of matter, the whole world would be no greater than a mathematical point.[65] For the whole has no other qualities than those of its parts, the qualities of which may be magnified quantitatively, as ten burners will have a greater heat capacity than one, but the synthesis does not create any new qualities. If, then, the constituent elements do not possess the quality of extension, how can their aggregate be extended? And if the aggregate is not extended either, then we would have a case of a whole being equal to its part, contrary to the well-known law that the whole is greater than its part.[66] This latter contention is not very convincing. A part may be taken in the physical-spatial sense like an inch in a yard of extensity, or in the spiritual-spaceless sense like the will in consciousness. Obviously we may say that volition is a part of our conscious life without being forced to say that our consciousness must be quantitatively greater than our volition. As soon as we ascend to the domain of spirit we must leave the whole category of magnitude behind. Now, adhering to Gabirol's own standpoint that an indivisible unit must be of a spiritual nature, we are not subjected, with regard to the aggregate of such units, to the physical law that the whole must be greater than its part. Gabirol's

[65] *Fons Vitae*, p. 52: 'Similiter etiam si posuerimus punctum esse partem corporis et corpus est compositum ex suis partibus, hoc est punctis quod tibi videtur; necesse est ut totalitas corporis non sit divisibilis quoniam partes eius indivisibiles sunt.'

[66] *Ibid.*, p. 57: 'Si duae partes coniunctae non fuerint pars divisibilis, ipsae duae tunc et pars una erunt aequales erunt ergo duo aequalia uni quod est inconveniens, similiter etiam dicendum de tertia et quarta parte, usque in infinitum. Sed si compositum ex omnibus fuerit pars una non divisibilis, hoc est, si plures partes sint aequales uni parti: ergo corpus totius mundi erit aequale uni suarum partium quae est indivisibilis.'

first contention, however, that if the atoms are conceived to lack the quality of extension, they cannot form in their aggregate any extended matter, for the synthesis does not give rise to any new qualities, is perfectly valid.

An equally strong defence for the theory of infinite divisibility was made by Maimonides in his *Guide*. He clings to the Aristotelian theory that a moving object must be divisible,[67] that an indivisible object must be immovable and hence immaterial. He shows the absurdity of the view that there is an atom which does not fill itself any definite place, and yet somehow or other keeps an atom of space occupied. The reader of general history of philosophy will here recall the Monads of Leibniz. Indeed, Munk has already called attention to a striking parallel to this view of the Mutakallimun, found in Leibniz's *Epistolae ad P. des Bosses*, where he remarks: 'Substantia nempe simplex etsi non habeat in se extensionem habet tamen positionem, quae est fundamentum extensionis.' Also one of the later Jewish thinkers, Joseph Albo, defines the point

---

[67] See Aristotle's *Physics*, VI, 7. He derives this idea that a movable object must be divisible from the conception of change of which locomotion is one type. Maimonides' formulation of the whole doctrine is as follows: כל משתנה מתחלק ולזה כל מתנועע מתחלק והוא גשם בהכרח וכל מה שלא יתחלק לא יתנועע ולזה אי אפשר שיהיה גשם כלל (see *Guide*, II, prop. 7). I did not connect, however, the idea that motion implies divisibility with the similar idea of change, for the reason that the latter was very much disputed both in Arabian as well as in Jewish circles. Some forms of change are apparently sudden and involve no divisibility. Personally, I think that the theory that a movable object must be divisible, is not dependent on the notion of change. It can be inferred from the *Physics*, VI, ch. 1, where it is argued that motion implies a front and a back side of the moving body, and anything that has two extremities is extended and divisible. This, indeed, is the way that Aaron of Nicomedia formulates it: שכל מתנועע יש לו קדימה ואחור ובהכרח יקבל החילוק. See *Eṣ Ḥayyim*, p. 7.

as beyond the category of space, but having position.[68] But how can a thing exist in the physical universe, not in a space garb? And how does a mathematical point monopolize a definite space when it is itself in no need of it? 'Such things', Maimonides therefore concludes, 'are only said; they exist only in words, not in thought, much less in reality.'[69] Another objection to the Mutakallimun's standpoint is how could we bisect a line composed of an odd number of atoms.[70] One might say that, since the atom has no magnitude, it is really of no consequence for an exact spatial division; but strangely enough, according to the Arabian thinkers, it has a magnitudinal value in conjunction; hence that side which will own this middle atom will be more extended than the other. Consequently an exact division in this case is impossible. This last argument was also advanced by Maimonides' imitator, Aaron of Nicomedia, the Karaite, in his work called *The Tree of Life*.[71]

Finally, the problem of infinite divisibility received a new treatment in the work entitled *The Wars of God*, by the acute thinker Levi b. Gerson, or Gersonides. He reiterates the idea that a thousand mathematical points could not produce anything more than a point.[72] He points out that matter has a property called continuity (*hitdabbekut*), by virtue of which it may be divided and subdivided *ad infinitum*, and the most infinitesimal parts

---

[68] *Dogmas*, p. 124. Compare, however, Isaac Israeli in his *Yesod Olam*, I, ch. 2, p. 3.

[69] See *Guide*, I, 51. This view of the Kalam is also stated in the Karaitic work, *The Tree of Life*, p. 13, comp. *FV.*, 65.

[70] *Guide*, I, ch. 73, third premise.

[71] See p. 7.

[72] *Milḥamot*, Leipzig, 1866, p. 345.

will still be extended and again continuous,[73] a view that coincides with the Kantian. But his most original contribution to the problem of infinite divisibility is his solution of Zeno's puzzle, thereby changing the whole meaning of the concept. We have seen how Saadya grappled with that puzzle and scarcely overcame it; we are now to see how Gersonides, four hundred years after, finally solved it— a solution well worth serious consideration on the part of present-day thinkers. Perhaps we had better let him talk for himself. He has just proved that the very notion of quantity in any of its forms, temporal or spatial, implies finitude and limitations, and he remarks:[74] ' Perhaps some one will question the argument just advanced, saying that there is one phase of quantity suggestive of the infinite, namely, the fact that number is infinitely augmentable and quantity is infinitely divisible; and it is also clear that quantity as such is infinitely augmentable, for it is not impossible that quantity as such should be greater than the universe. True, there is something that prevents the possibility of having matter larger than the universe, namely, the fact that there is no space beyond the universe, as the *Philosopher* (i.e. Aristotle) has shown; but it is not impossible for matter as such. . . . Our answer is that it is evident after a little thought that this objection is unable to overthrow our premise which we have laid down before, namely, that quantity as such is of necessity finite, for the nature of quantity necessitates finitude, as already explained. *But the endlessness that we find as characteristic of number and extensity is not endlessness in quantity, but endlessness in the process of division and augmentation.* That is to say, much as you divide it, the

[73] *Ibid.*, p. 333, also p. 346.   [74] *Ibid.*, pp. 333-4.

capacity will still be left for further subdivision; and much as you augment it, the capacity will still be left of further augmentation. Yet divide and augment as you may, you will always have quantitative finitude, for number does not have such power as to change into non-number (i.e. infinite), but it does have the power to change into greater numbers. Thus it can never turn into an infinite, for it has been already explained that number is finite. The same is true of extensity. . . . And from this explanation it will become clear that extensity has no infinite number of parts whether potentially or actually, for if it had an infinite number of parts potentially or actually, a great absurdity would follow, namely, that a given finite extensity would be infinite, for that which is composed of an infinite number of parts must be infinite in extensity, for any one of these potential parts has of necessity some quantity, for extensity cannot be divided into non-extensity; and it is evident that, however minute the extensity each one of the infinite parts may have, the whole will certainly be infinite in extensity. . . . Hence what we mean by saying that extensity is infinitely divisible is that each part retains the possibility of being subdivided, though the number of parts always remains finite.'

This whole discussion involves Gersonides' great contribution to the notion of the infinite—which will be discussed in a later chapter. The keynote of the argument however is clear, namely, that infinite divisibility is not a state but a process, not an accomplished fact; for it is ridiculous to speak of an ended endless series, but the unlimited possibility of dividing and subdividing extensity into smaller extensities. And if one were to live thousands of years and were constantly engaged in dividing and crumbling a piece of matter, with unimaginably fine instruments, he would have at the end of that time an unthinkably great number of particles of course, but it would be a finite number nevertheless. Prolong the life of that miserable man, and the world would be enriched by so many more particles, but the sum total will be finite again. The number of grains of sand on the shore of the sea is overwhelming; but it is a definite and finite number. It is absurd and contradictory to speak of an existing infinite number. Infinite divisibility denotes a process, but not a state. Such is the solution of Gersonides. It rids us at once of the haunting ghost of Zeno which continued to appear as soon as we had infinite divisibility on our lips. Gersonides showed us how to make of it an intelligible theory.

We are now ready to draw a line under the first general inquiry of our work. The problems that so far occupied our attention are connected with the conception of empirical space, i.e. with that part of space which has embodied itself in concrete tangible matter, and has become therefore an object of experience. We have seen how the Jewish thinkers never doubted the independent objective reality of space as presented to their senses. They differed as to its ontological importance in the make-up of things, they took issues as to its accidental or substantial nature, but no one questioned its independent existence. Thus the Kantian view of the subjectivity of space, which puts all extensity at the mercy of our senses, is far removed from the Jewish standpoint. Some thinkers, we have seen, even go to the extreme in maintaining that space is the sum and substance of all material existence, the substantial groundwork of all things. Perhaps this distinctly empirical standpoint is somewhat responsible for the general Jewish opposition to Arabian atomism with its assumption of a real yet spaceless particle as the basis of the material world. At any rate, Jewish thinkers all upheld the indestructibility of extension by means of division, that space is infinitely divisible—a theory the tremendous difficulties of which were altogether removed by Gersonides, who showed that the notion of infinite divisibility denotes a process rather than a state.

CHAPTER II

ABSOLUTE SPACE

THE subject that now presents itself for discussion, is *absolute space*, by which I mean not the space of this or that object that is directly given in our intuition, but the one that is the product of a mental process of abstraction and generalization. The former space is concrete and perceptual, denoting an impress of the external world upon our senses; the latter space is absolute and conceptual, denoting a reaction of the mind upon the external world. Empirical space is variegated and discrete, manifesting itself in the space of this desk and that landscape and those heavens; conceptual space is uniform and continuous—one great *continuum* without bounds. The conception is a difficult one, implying the absence of any material data to which the human mind could cling: that is why it was so often a source of error and confusion. Yet if you close your eyes and think away the walls of the room and the furniture in it; and think away the world outside of your room, the sun, the moon, and the stars; and think away also the earth under your feet, and the very body in which your mind happens to reside; and think only of your mind floating in an endless monotonous void—you will have some faint glimpse of the endless *continuum* in which the material universe is conceived to be submerged, absolute space.

We have seen in the preceding chapter that Jewish mediaeval thinkers never questioned the reality of the extensity of things, never doubted the independent, objective existence of empirical space; yet up till the end of the fourteenth century they all unanimously repudiated the assumption of absolute space. This can be explained in two ways. First of all empiricism was the standpoint taken by the Jewish philosophers in the middle ages. It is proclaimed by Saadya in the introduction to his book called *Beliefs and Opinions*, and it is emphasized by the thinkers that came after him. Maimonides scoffs at the Mutakallimun, those Arabian scholastics, who would assume anything imaginable which would fit in the system; and if contradicted by our senses, they would have a ready reply: human perception is not reliable.[75] Hence this empirical standpoint might have prevented the Jewish thinkers from believing the existence of anything that cannot be empirically known. But there is also another reason that has an equal degree of probability. Aristotle's conception of space was such as to exclude the notion of absolute space. Now Aristotelianism exercised unimaginable sway over the Jewish thinkers. It was the standard of truth. Thus if the Bible took issues with Aristotle, it was incumbent upon them to explain away the apparent meaning of the Bible, and so interpret it as to be in accord with Aristotle. 'Stultum est dicere Aristotelem errasse.' Hence in accepting the Aristotelian notion of space, which, as I say, excluded the reality of absolute space, they had

---

[75] Comp. *Guide*, I, ch. 73, prop. 10.

to accept also the conclusion that might be logically drawn therefrom. And so the situation lasted until the Aristotelian influence began to wane, and the great challenger of Aristotle, Hasdai Crescas, appeared, and gave to the notion of space a different meaning, and proved the objective reality of absolute space. Let us first discuss the history of the Aristotelian notion of space in Jewish philosophy, we will then come to the objective reality of that vast *continuum* which we cannot experience, but which the mind postulates.

I. Just a word is necessary to call up in the reader's mind this Aristotelian notion which we have already discussed in the introduction at length. We all speak of things being in space; the desk, the house, the aeroplane, the world—all things are in space. Space then carries the notion of an encompassing body, and Aristotle defined it as *the first limit of the containing body*. Now the far-reaching consequences of this definition lie in the fact that it does away with the mysterious independent existence of space. It is simply the relation of contiguity between two objects; where this contiguity is missing, of course you have no space. Thus the uppermost, all-encompassing sphere in the Ptolemaic astronomy, while being the space of all things, is itself in no space; for there is nothing higher to be in contact with it, not even a void.

This Aristotelian notion was, as I said, accepted without reserve. Saadya[76] combats the view of space as that in

[76] *Emunot*, I, 4: או שמא יחשוב במקום הארץ ויאמר אי זה דבר היה במקום הזה ומאמרו זה אמנם מביא אותו סכלותו בגדר המקום. וסברתו כי ענין המקום הוא מה שהוא מושם תחת הדברים ותבקש נפשו מקום למקום ורואה שאין לזה תכלית ויהיה נבוך. וצריך שאבאר כי אמתת המקום איננו כמו שחשב אבל הוא פגישת שני הגשמים המתמששים ויקרא

which all things are submerged, and defines it as 'the contiguity between two objects'. He thus answers the objection levelled at the adherents of the doctrine of *creatio ex nihilo*, namely, what was there in the space of the world before it had been created? Since there was no world, there was no relation of contiguity, and hence no space. He also meets Zeno's argument that if all things are in space, space itself will have to be in space, and so on *ad infinitum*, consequently space does not exist. The strength of this argument is evidently questionable; all it may prove is that space is infinite, but not that it is non-existent. To Saadya, however, such a conclusion would not be in accord with Aristotelianism, and hence wrong. He shows that if

מקום משושם מקום אבל ישוב כל אחד מהם מקום לחברו. והארץ עתה בסבובה קצתה מקום לקצתה וכאשר לא תהיה ארץ ולא נשמים יבטל שיאמר מקום בשום פנים.

Kaufmann in his *Attributenlehre*, p. 63, note 117, misconstrued the whole passage. He explains the phrase מה שהוא מושם תחת הדברים, which he wrongly designates as Saadya's own view—as 'dasjenige was an die Stelle der Dinge sich setzt, d.h. beim Fortrücken eines Dings dafür eintritt'. When an immersed body, a cubic inch in volume, is removed, the liquid will naturally fill the gap, the cubic inch of the liquid being the space of the displaced body. But according to this interpretation, an object and its space cannot be conceived simultaneously; which is absurd. To place an object and to displace it, are two distinct ideas. Perhaps what Kaufmann had in mind is not the cubic inch of the displacing liquid, but the cubic inch as such, the stereometric content, so that the interval between the superficies of an object would be its space, a theory discussed and combated in Aristotle's *Physics*; but this 'interval' is altogether wanting in the words of the definition. What Saadya referred to in that expression is undoubtedly the Platonic notion of an all-containing receptacle, against which Saadya advances Zeno's argument that this receptacle must itself be contained, and so *ad infinitum*. Kaufmann also misunderstood the expression אבל יָשׁוּב כל אחד מהם מקום לחברו, apparently he read יִשּׁוּב, for he translates it: 'Die Ausdehnung—eigentlich das von jedem von beiden Bewohnte', but the Arabic original, يصير, clearly indicates the true meaning.

you understand by space a mere relation of contiguity, the whole argument becomes meaningless. But the reader will realize at once that this position, while apparently attacking Zeno, really admits his argument, i.e. that space as an all-encompassing void is inconceivable ; there is only a relation of contiguity. There is *place*, but not *space*.

This became the traditional view in Jewish philosophy. Gabirol speaks of space as implying 'the immediacy of the surface of one body to that of another body', or simply 'the contact between two bodies'.[77] Abraham bar Ḥiyya defines space as 'that which envelopes the shape of a body all around from the outside'[78]—a phraseology which is not quite fortunate, but whose meaning is clear. Joseph Ibn Zaddik maintains that 'the true meaning of space is propinquity, for there is no container without something contained, nor anything contained without a container',[79] and that 'the uppermost sphere needs no space because its parts constitute space for one another',[80] which means that the largest diurnal sphere, inasmuch as it rotates only around its axis, and does not as a whole change its position, does not require any space over and above ; only its parts change their relative position, and they constitute space for one another. Abraham Ibn Daud understands by space 'that

[77] See *Fons Vitae*, II, 14, p. 74, 24 'Locus est applicatio superficiei corporis ad superficiem corporis alterius'; comp. also II, 14, p 49, 5 'Intentio loci noti est applicatio duorum corporum.' Comp. *Meḳor Ḥayyim*, II, 21 : היות המקום יחייב דבקות שטח גוף בשטח גוף אחר, also II, 23, 33.

[78] See *Hegyon Hanefesh*, p. 3: כי המקום הוא דבר חופה את צלם הגוף מכל סביבותיה מבחוץ.

[79] *Microcosm*, p. 15 : שאמתת המקום וענינו שהוא סמוך לפי שאין מקום מבלי מתקומם אין מתקוממם בלי מקום.

[80] *Ibid.*, p. 11 : ועל כן אין צריך למקום שכל חלק ממנו מקום לחברו. Cf. *Phys.*, IV, 6.

EF. F

the surfaces of which compass the object that is in it'.[81] Aaron of Nicomedia, the Karaite, writes: 'The primary meaning of space is that which matter occupies, the dimensions of the spatial body being called space. It also denotes unoccupied dimensions or the whole space. And thinkers are at issue in this matter. Some apply the term space to that which is in contact with the surface of the body and surrounds it on all sides, others apply it to the void that embraces the universe; and the first opinion is the correct one.'[82] Finally, Gersonides takes the same standpoint when he argues that 'above and below relations are not due to any mathematical dimensions, but to the things that bear these relations. Thus light objects move upwards, heavy ones downwards; and when there was nothing light or heavy these above and below relations did not exist'.[83]

Thus we have seen how the Aristotelian conception of space acquired the certainty of a philosophical tradition. Jewish philosophers used it as a self-evident truism, as a logical foundation for the doctrine of *creatio ex nihilo* and other important theological doctrines, and it occurred to no one to question the validity of this foundation. Then Hasdai Crescas appeared, free from the hypnotism of the Greek master, and with a boldness that we must admire, considering the circumstances, commenced to challenge Aristotelian doctrines, including the one concerning space, and his challenge resounds in the *Dogmas* of his disciple Joseph Albo, and even in the works of Don Isaac Abrabanel by no means an independent thinker. Perhaps it was

---

[81] *Emunah Ramah*, p. 16: שכל מה שהוא במקום שטחי מקומו בופים עליו. Perhaps it should read חופים. Comp. the quotation from *Hegyon Hanefesh* in note 78.

[82] *Eṣ Ḥayyim*, ch. 20.   [83] *Milḥamot*, p. 371.

this challenge of Aristotelianism that marked the beginning of the end of the mediaeval period in Jewish philosophy.[84]

Crescas finds four difficulties in the Aristotelian notion of space, which he formulates very laconically, as 'the encompassing, equal, and separate surface'.[85] These 'difficulties' are not very difficult. First of all, he argues, the all-encompassing sphere, having no container is, according to Aristotle, in no space; but all things have their existence in space. Consequently, Aristotle is wrong. Secondly, Aristotle taught that every element has a certain affinity towards a particular place at which it is at rest and to which it is in motion. Thus air is naturally at rest in the concavity of the celestial layer of fire; everywhere else it can be at rest only by means of some external force. Now if this be true, it would follow that either the inner parts of the air will never be in their natural place, not being in contact with the concave surface of fire to which they strive as parts of the air element, or else their natural place is different from that of the whole—either of which alternative

---

[84] The reader should not assume, however, that Aristotelian influences disappear altogether from Jewish thought. Even a Kabbalist like Moses Botarel speaks of Aristotle in laudatory terms and accords him a seat in Paradise. See his commentary on the *Book of Creation*, p. 26, quoted in Steinschneider's *Hebraische Uebersetzungen*, p. 269. But the name of the 'Philosopher' no longer enjoyed universal and unquestionable authority. Thus Isaac Abrabanel, though often accepting Aristotelian notions, dares to confer upon him the epithet 'Ancient Serpent'; see his מפעלות אלהים, II, 3.

[85] See *Or Adonai*, ed. Vienna, 1860, p. 6, where the definition of space is formulated: היות המקום השטח המקיף השוה הנבדל. Comp. Narboni on *Guide*, I, 73, prop. 2, where he speaks of התכלית המקיף השוה הנבדל. On p. 15 Crescas advances four arguments against this Aristotelian definition. Compare also *Minḥat Kenaot*, by R. Jeḥiel of Pisa, p. 26 : (i.e. of space) שגדרו הוא תבלית הגשם המקיף במתקומם הנוגע בו.

is absurd. Thirdly, how do the celestial bodies move in a circle, what place is the goal of *their* striving? Fourthly, Aristotle held that a rotating ball has its place, though accidental, in the axis which does not move; now if the axis is meant to be a material part of the ball, it is evident that motion in this case would be impossible without a disintegration of its parts, and if it is meant to be a mere geometrical line that can be drawn through the centre, it cannot be the place of the object.

These arguments are by no means convincing. Besides, they are not altogether relevant. They do not exactly 'hit the mark'. Crescas is more aggressive and much more convincing in the concrete problem of the void, which outgrows from this whole discussion, and which I reserved for later treatment. I shall therefore let these arguments pass without criticism. It should, however, be remarked that Albo also advances four arguments against the Aristotelian notion, the first two of which are identical with the first two arguments of Crescas.[86] Albo's other two arguments are as follows: According to Aristotle, the place of a part would be greater than the place of the whole, for a spherical body in which a deep break has been made will require a greater surface to contain it inside and outside than when it was whole. Thus let figure 1 represent a ball, and let figure 2 represent the same ball but in which a deep wedge-like hole has been hollowed out, and let the thread in both cases represent the Aristotelian 'container' or place. It is evident that figure 2 is only a part of figure 1, and yet it takes a greater thread to embrace the second ball than the first, because geometrically AOB is greater than AB. Consequently a part would occupy

---

[86] See *Dogmas*, II, 17. See also ספר הגדרים, *s. v.*

ABSOLUTE SPACE

a greater place than the whole, which is absurd. The second argument is a similar one. Take a body which occupies a certain amount of Aristotelian space—or let us call it for brevity's sake, place—and divide it; since each segregated part now requires a containing surface for itself, the total amount of place occupied by that body will now be greater. The further you divide, the greater the place that it will occupy, which contradicts the Euclidean law

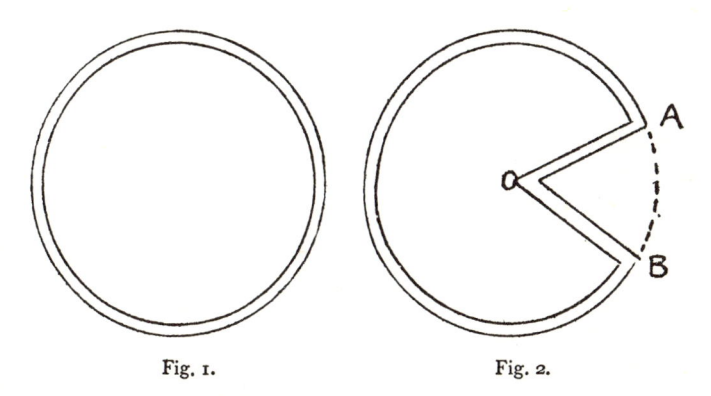

Fig. 1.　　　　　　Fig. 2.

that equal bodies occupy equal spaces. These two arguments also are easily met by the idea that the Euclidean law of space cannot be applied to place.

To come back to Crescas, what was his own view of space? According to his conception, it is a great *continuum*, an infinite and immovable void, ready to receive material objects. And in receiving matter, it is not displaced, for it is immovable, but on the contrary it embodies itself in it and becomes concrete extensity, or, as Aristotle called it, the interval between the extremities of an object.[87]

---

[87] See *Or Adonai*, p. 15 b: שהמקום האמיתי לדבר הוא רוחק אשר בין תכליות המקיף והשקרים אשר חייב אריסטו לזה הדעת אין ענין להם ... See also 17 b. According to Simplicius, Plato defined space as

Aristotle rejected that view for the reason that all bodies move in space, and if the interval of a body were space in itself, we would have space moving in space. To this Crescas answers, there are no various spaces. *It is one infinite and immovable.* When matter is immersed in space it is like a net in a stagnant pool, which when moving does not disturb the silent waters. In other words, extensity and void are not two kinds of space, but really one; only the former has had an admixture of matter and has therefore visualized itself, while the latter is pure and hence invisible. Extended matter is like a streak of sunlight that has become visible by absorbing particles of dust. Thus we have no phenomenon of space moving in space. Empirical space and absolute space are one—this is the great idea of Hasdai Crescas.

Crescas found a faithful follower in Joseph Albo, who incorporated this conception of space in his *Dogmas*, but Albo seems to have been his first and last follower. Conditions in Spain, for some four centuries an asylum of Jewish culture, were no longer favourable for the development of free thought. The end of the fifteenth century found Spanish Jewry subjected to persecution and dire oppression, which strangled the zeal for genuine speculation in the Jewish breast and brought the progress of Jewish philosophy to such an abrupt end. It is, however, to the credit of the Jew's yearning for knowledge that even in those dreadful times a man like Don Isaac Abrabanel, one of the foremost statesmen of Spain, but later an outcast of the land which he faithfully served, found moments of leisure in the intermissions of his aimless wandering to

τὸ διάστημα τὸ μεταξὺ τῶν ἐσχάτων τοῦ περιέχοντος (Simpl., *Phys.*, IV, p. 571). If Simplicius is correct, Crescas takes the Platonic standpoint.

compose philosophical treatises which, though wanting in originality, display a vast amount of erudition and acquaintance with philosophical systems. In the question under discussion he does not side with Crescas, but adopts the Aristotelian conception of space.[88]

II. The preceding discussion as to whether we are to understand by space a material receptacle or an unlimited *continuum*, is altogether useless, if not supplemented with a discussion of a problem which is implied therein, namely, the existence of a void. The Aristotelian conception involves a cosmology which admits of no void. The universe is composed of spheres one within the other, all compact, with no space between. The innermost sphere, sphere A, has its place in the concave form of sphere B, and sphere B in sphere C, and so forth. The uppermost all-containing sphere is in no place: it is the limit of the universe. Thus there is place; but no pure space, no void, whether between things or outside of them. On the other hand, if we mean by space an unlimited *continuum* embodied here and there in a concrete material object, a canvas as it were in which some fine tapestry is woven, we naturally postulate the existence of an unembodied space or a void. Thus so long as the Jewish thinkers unquestioningly accepted the Aristotelian notion of space, they discarded the possibility of a void; it was Crescas who first endeavoured to prove that the void is a real fact.

It is noteworthy that the existence of a void was one of the great issues between mediaeval Aristotelianism and Arabian scholasticism or the Kalam; the former, as we have seen, vigorously renouncing it, and the latter vigorously

[88] אשר הוא שטה הדבר המקיף שוה נברל : IV, 3, מפעלות אלהים
למקומם כפי מה שנדרו אריסטו.

maintaining it. The Mutakallimun maintained the void, because it is an indispensable element in any system which resolves matter into segregated particles of minute magnitude generating all phenomena by their motion.[89] Jewish thinkers, we have found, were averse to atomism; so that the postulation of a void was no requisite of their system. At all events, Jewish philosophy before Crescas was unanimously against the existence of pure space.[90] Let us see some of its chief reasons.

Joseph ibn Zaddik offers a proof from nature. Take a pitcher and plunge it into water with its mouth upside down. No water will come in the pitcher. Remove the air, and the water will instantly rush into it, so as not to leave a vacuum. Or take a jar with a perforated bottom, fill it with water; of course the water will issue through the bottom, and air will enter through the top, and immediately fill the gap. Now fill the jar with water again, and close it so tightly as to leave no access to the air; no drop of water will leak through the pores of the bottom. This clearly shows that there is no vacuum in nature.[91] The argument, by the way, is Aristotelian, and is also cited by Narboni.[92]

How then is motion possible if there is no empty space? In a compact world of matter, where even elbow-room is denied us, how can we move? Ibn Zaddik adopts the Aristotelian answer. The air is very elastic, being

---

[89] See *Guide*, I, 73, prop. 2.

[90] Abraham Ibn Ezra is perhaps an exception to this statement. He nowhere posits the void, but one might infer it from the atomistic ideas that he expresses in the fragments called ערוגת החכמה ופרדס המזמה. See above, note 55.

[91] *Microcosm*, p. 16.

[92] See Narboni on *Guide*, I, 73, prop. 3.

easily condensed and rarefied. And when we press forward, we set up a system of condensation before us, and a system of rarefaction behind us. Even the removal of a drop of water thus affects the whole universe; but no vacuum is anywhere formed.[93] The reader will realize that, as Narboni rightly remarked,[94] the atomists could not have taken the same view in explaining atomic motion by condensation and rarefaction without being compelled to assume the existence of a void, because the atom is conceived to be an indivisible, non-magnitudinal and ultimate reality, and hence can neither swell nor shrink.

A similar argument for the non-existence of the vacuum is adduced by Maimonides from the science of hydraulics.[95] Water is being carried from a lower to a higher level by means of a pump out of which the air has been exhausted, the underlying principle being that 'nature abhors a vacuum', that it tends to fill an empty space as soon as it is formed.

An altogether original argument was suggested by the Kabbalist, Isaac Ibn Latif.[96] A visual sensation of light implies a certain gas medium through which radiant energy is being propagated in waves, finally impinging the retina of our eye, thus producing a sensation. Ibn Latif was of course ignorant of the modern undulatory theory of light; instead, he believed that an object of light emits certain material corpuscles—similar to the now repudiated Newtonian conception. But at all events a certain medium is required through which the radiant energy or the radiant corpuscles are transferred. Hence our vision of the luminary bodies proves the total absence of intervening

---

[93] *Microcosm*, p. 16.
[94] *l. c.*, I, 73, prop. 2.
[95] *Ibid.*, prop. 3.
[96] See רב פעלים, section 60.

vacuum. It is curious, however, that in the end he remarks as follows: '... and the very same demonstration for the non-existence of the void, is a demonstration for its existence; and understand this, for it is sealed.' How this argument also proves the reality of a void is not easy to guess, unless he meant that the radiant waves in order to move must have free space—a contention which, as we have seen, has already been refuted by earlier thinkers. But the argument in itself is noteworthy.

The reasons so far advanced are drawn from the realm of nature, and all they may prove is that there are no empty interstices between the material objects, that the equilibrium of the world demands a filling up of all gaps, leaving nothing empty. They demonstrate the familiar maxim: 'Nature abhors a vacuum'. Of course, as Solomon Maimon, the Kantian interpreter of Maimonism, correctly suggested, nature does not exactly *abhor* a vacuum, it is *forced* to fill it; that is to say, a vacuum is a *natural* existence, only it is obviated by external forces. When the air is exhausted from the tube, the water is forced into it by the atmospheric pressure; so that when the tube is too high for the atmospheric pressure to raise the water, a void will *naturally* form in the tube. This physical phenomenon was entirely overlooked by the men I have mentioned. The mediaeval term *horror vacui* is really misleading. At all events, those arguments tend to refute the existence of void within the material realm, or, following the analogy of our previous terminology, *empirical void*, which does not mean an experience of a void, but a void of experience, or a blank in the midst of objects that appeal to our sensation. Now what of *absolute void*, what of pure infinite dimensionality in which the universe is supposed to exist, is it real or fictitious? Is there any space beyond the confines of the world? Or let us imagine matter annihilated or non-existent, would there be space after all?

Gersonides answers these questions negatively. Tridimensionality is a quality of matter; take away matter and you have no space. It is absurd to say that before the creation of the tangible world there was pure space; for if so, why did God create the world in this part of the infinite void and not in another? The void is alike in all its parts, no one of which owns a greater possibility of being informed and embodied than another. If then you assume a void, you have to assume logically a coextensive infinite matter, which is likewise absurd. Hence pre-existent space is an impossibility.[97] The argument is based on the theory of creationism, a theory no longer tenable in philosophical circles; but the whole question about the *pre-existence* of space is a scholastic one. Gersonides, however, goes a step further, and endeavours to show that any form of empty space is inconceivable. There is a patent contradiction involved in the term 'empty space'. Space, we know, is measurable and infinitely divisible. But empty space means that there is nothing existent, in short, nothingness, and how can we conceive of nothingness as measurable or divisible, or of one nothingness as greater than another? Consequently empty space is an *absurdum*. The argument hides a certain fallacy, but let us go on and see the concrete example which he offers in order to demonstrate the absurdity of the void. Imagine two bodies separated by empty space, one $ABCD$ and the other $EFGH$, placed in two positions, the lines AB and EF in one position being parallel lines, and oblique in the other.

[97] See *Milḥamot*, p. 365.

76 PROBLEM OF SPACE IN JEWISH PHILOSOPHY

Now in Figure 1 we say that the intervening distance or void represented by AE equals BF; while in Figure 2 we say AE is greater than BF. But both AE and BF do not represent any material existence, consequently they are zero, and how can zero be a basis of comparison, and above all how can one zero be greater than another? Hence the void is an absurdity.—Q.E.D.[98] But it is evident that Gersonides plays hide-and-seek with the notion of pure space. This term stands for mere dimensionality devoid

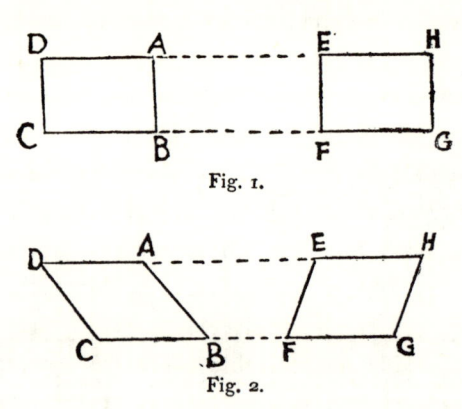

Fig. 1.

Fig. 2.

of any material thing. Now if one were to count things, he would of course have to leave out the void, and consider it mathematically zero. But here it is not the counting of the two bodies that is involved, but the *extension* of the intervening void; and from the point of view of extension, the void is a definite quantity unless it has been previously demonstrated that the void is an impossibility—something that is here to be proved. Gersonides, therefore, in assuming that the lines of extension AE and BF are zero, is clearly arguing in a circle.

Gersonides, however, concludes that the void is an

[98] *Ibid.*, pp. 378 and 379.

illusion. It is strange that such an acute thinker should fall into such an open fallacy; perhaps it was the Aristotelian system to which he mainly clung that required of him such a conclusion, and the need of a conclusion blinded him to the validity of the reasoning. Reason is very often sacrificed in order to suit a system. At any rate, Gersonides firmly held that the universe is finite; that there is no space beyond the world. But here a logical puzzle presented itself to his mind. 'There is no space beyond the world', but does not the very word 'beyond' suggest space? Does it not convey the notion of outstretched plains, even while this is meant to be denied. Let us expand that brief statement; do we not mean that there is no space in the space beyond the world? Is not therefore the whole idea about the finitude of space meaningless and erroneous? Gersonides, however, does not despair. The puzzle is not real, but linguistic. Human language fits our daily needs, but is not rich enough to express many a fine shading in reality. It is incapable to express the absolute absence of space in terms of before and after, just as it is incapable to express the absolute non-existence of time in the relations of before and after. When we say, what was *before* the beginning of time? we experience the same difficulty. It is not however real, but simply verbal, due to the inadequacy of language.[99] This is Gersonides's solution of the puzzle. Some five centuries after, Kant also grappled with this puzzle, but his solution was different. We can conceive no end to space, no limits beyond which there is no space. Hence space must be a necessity of thought, a form of intention. Which solution is saner this is not the place to discuss.

[99] *Ibid.*, p. 384.

So much for the negative side of this void-discussion. This side, it should be noted, does not make out a very impressive case. Its reasoning is sometimes hackneyed, and sometimes faulty. Judah Halevi counted the void as one of the things that common sense seems to accept, and syllogistic reasoning rejects;[100] but he did not show us what this 'syllogistic reasoning' is. Yet although the proposition which this side attempted to put forth had no great intrinsic force, it had that force which is in every view that coincides with tradition. It traced back its lineage to Aristotle. *Ipse dixit.* That is why this negative view was popular in Jewish philosophy for so long a time. At last the affirmative side appears on the scene, represented by one man only, radical, bold, and daring—Hasdai Crescas. Let us hear what he has to say.

Crescas does not enter into a detailed discussion with the followers of Aristotle, he attacks straightway Aristotle himself. Incidentally he points out the absurdity of Gersonides's difficulty with empty space as a magnitude. If you remove the air from a jar, you do not remove extension along with it. And the empty extension in the jar is of course measurable and divisible.[101] He also shows in passing that finite space is inconceivable, because what is there beyond?[102] Crescas evidently rejects Gersonides's explanation by an appeal to linguistic poverty. He also clears another difficulty that Gersonides had in connexion with the void, namely, the void is the same in all its parts, why then did God create the finite world in this part of the infinite void rather than in another? Crescas answers that

[100] *Cosari*, III, 49: כאשר תרהיק המחשבה והסברה העדר הרקות והקשות השבליות מחיבות זה.

[101] See *Or Adonai*, p. 15 a.   [102] *Ibid.*

just because the void is the same in all its parts it is absurd to ask why God should have created the world in another part rather than in this.[103] His main charge, however, Crescas concentrates on Aristotle himself. He examines his arguments singly and discloses their weakness. We will follow the order of his treatment.

1. If void existed, says Aristotle, there would be no motion. For motion is either natural or forced; natural motion being that of a body moving *to* the place to which it has affinity, as an apple moving downwards, and forced motion being that of a body moving *away from* the place of its affinity, as when an apple moves upwards. But a void is *mitdammeh hahalakim*, the same in all its parts, no one of which can enjoy the special affinity of an object. Hence natural motion in a void is absurd. And since it is implied in forced motion the latter is also absurd. Moreover, imagine an arrow hurled from a bow-string; now ordinarily the arrow moves on by virtue of the fact that the air which has also received a violent attack from the bow-string becomes a propelling power for the arrow. Now in a void where such a propelling power is lacking, we should expect that no matter how much the string is strained, the arrow should powerlessly fall down, as soon as it leaves the string. Thus motion in any of its forms is impossible in a void, and hence the void cannot be conceived to exist. Thus, instead of maintaining that motion is impossible *without* empty space, the true idea is that motion is impossible *with* empty space.

To this Crescas replies: The fault of this argument is chiefly in failing to realize that the void is not considered by its adherents to be the *cause* of motion, but only the

[103] *Ibid.*, p. 70 a.

medium. The argument seeks to disprove the idea that the void is cause—an idea maintained by no one. Aristotle argues that the void cannot bear any special attraction to any body, and since that attraction is the basis of motion, the latter is inconceivable in a vacuum. But no one claimed that it does have any peculiar attraction. Gersonides has already remarked that the notions of 'upward' and 'downward' are not due to mere mathematical dimensions, but to the objects that may be up or down. The fire does not seek any mathematical dimensions above it, but the concave lunar surface. Thus it is not the void that exercises any attraction or repulsion, but the bodies in it. The earth attracts the apple, and there may be an intervening void, yet that does not hinder motion, but on the contrary helps it, serving as a free medium. Indeed, the whole Aristotelian position is questionable. *A medium is no requisite for motion.* It hinders it; the rarer the medium, the freer the movement. Light objects move upwards, and heavy objects move downwards, or rather—and here a very important physical theory occurs to his mind—*all bodies move downwards*, only, the lighter bodies are pressed upwards by heavier downward moving bodies. And all this goes on without necessitating a material medium which is really an obstacle and a hindrance for a moving body. It is the void which is the true medium for the free exercise of motion.[104]

2. The second and third arguments of Aristotle are treated by Crescas simultaneously. Motion, speaking mathematically, is a function of two variables: the medium and the motive force. Let us see the medium-variable first. The velocity of a body is proportioned to the

[104] *Ibid.*, p. 14 a ff.

medium: the rarer the medium, the quicker the motion. If we could imagine a medium of an infinitely rare density, then, all other things being equal, the body would move in an infinitesimal time. But the void has altogether no density, hence a body will move therein in no time at all. But this is absurd, for the distance in which the body moves is divisible, it is a succession of points; and the moving body 'must take its time', it cannot come to the second point before it passes the first, and when it is on the second point, it is not yet on the third. Hence even this 'champion racer' must take cognizance in its movement of the relations of before and after, and consequently must take up some time after all. Therefore the void is an impossibility.

The impossibility of an absolutely timeless movement is further corroborated when we come to examine the second variable of motion, i.e. the motive force, which forms Aristotle's third argument. The velocity of a body is, all other things being equal, directly proportional to the propelling power: the stronger that power, the swifter the motion. This law holds true in the hurling of a weight upward in the air, as well as downwards in the water, and we should expect it to hold good also in the case of a vacuum. But in accordance with the law of the first variable, a body moves through a void under a given force in no time. Now double that force, and the velocity will have to be doubled too. But what can be quicker than timeless motion? Hence, Aristotle concludes, the void is an impossibility and an absurdity.[105]

To these two arguments Crescas replies: A body that is impelled to move by a certain force acquires a certain

[105] p. 5 a.

'fundamental velocity'; that is to say, a fundamental capacity to move a certain distance within a certain time unimpeded by any medium like water or gas. When that body happens to meet a medium, its velocity is slackened of course. The denser the medium, the slower the movement. Remove the medium, and the body will resume its initial 'fundamental velocity'. Thus the law that the velocity of a body is inversely proportional to the density of the medium is not a true statement of fact. Represent it mathematically, and you have

$$\frac{V}{V'} = \frac{D'}{D}; \quad V' = \frac{DV}{D'}.$$

But the density of the void (D') equals zero, hence

$$V' = \frac{DV}{0} = \infty.$$

Thus the velocity of a body moving in a vacuum is infinite, which is absurd, as Aristotle himself has shown. But this whole mathematical formula is untenable. The true law is *that the slackening of the 'fundamental velocity' of a given body is directly proportional to the density of the medium.* Thus representing the slackened progress by S, we have

$$\frac{S}{S'} = \frac{D}{D'}; \quad S' = \frac{SD'}{D}; \text{ but } D' = 0, \therefore S' = 0.$$

In other words, a body moving in a vacuum, not being impeded by any medium, will move according to its 'fundamental velocity'. It is just as unwise to argue that inasmuch as a body moves swifter in a light medium than in a dense, it will move in a void in no time at all, as it is to maintain that because a man that is less tired will move faster than a man that is more tired, a man that is not tired at all will move altogether in no time. Both statements leave out of consideration the principle of the fundamental natural velocity.[106]

3. The fourth argument of Aristotle is as follows: The void is conceived as mere tridimensionality, ready to receive material objects, the dimensions of the thing uniting with the dimensions of the void, and forming one. But how is it possible? How can two ells form one ell? And if it is possible in the case of matter and void, why should it be impossible in the case of matter and matter? We will thus have to suspend the law of impenetrability, for the reason why two bodies cannot occupy the same space at the same time, is not because they are black or warm or in any other way qualified, but because they have dimensions. And yet some assume that a body can penetrate a void which is spatiality itself. If then this were true, there should be an equal possibility of compressing two or more material bodies into one, and we should thus be enabled to compress the whole universe into a tiny insignificant speck. Thus the assumption of the void leads us into monstrous absurdities.[107]

To this Crescas replied: Two things cannot occupy the same space in the same time, not because each one of them has its own dimensions, but because each one has *dimensional matter*. In other words, in order that a body should be impenetrable it must have two things combined: spatiality and corporeality. And just as unextended matter, if such a thing were conceivable, would not be impenetrable, so spatiality devoid of matter could not resist the intrusion of a material body. That is why an ell of matter and an ell of a void can so combine as to form one. Crescas

[106] *Ibid.*, p. 14 b.   [107] *Ibid.*, p. 5 a.

herewith also replies to Zeno's argument that if space were real, it would be in space; for all things real are in space, and so on *ad infinitum*. It is only material spatiality that occupies and monopolizes a certain space so as not to admit any other body to immigrate into its domain; pure spatiality has no policy to refuse immigration, on the contrary, it bids welcome to any object that seeks to settle within its borders. Hence the void does not strictly speaking 'occupy' space, and is always ready to be intruded as long as it has not been invested with corporeality.[108]

Such were the refutations that Crescas hurled against the Aristotelian position. The reader will undoubtedly be impressed by the soundness of the argument, as well as by his turning his back on Aristotelian physical notions, and catching glimpses of the modern science of physics. We may nowadays repudiate the possibility of an absolute void and claim that there is an all-filling and all-penetrating ether, but the existence of ether is after all only a hypothesis. Empirically the void is by no means denied. It should also be noted that while the Mutakallimun postulated the existence of a void merely to suit their atomic system, Crescas who did not adopt the atomic standpoint takes a different course. He first disproves the seemingly convincing Aristotelian arguments, and having removed by sound reasoning the traditional prejudice, he shows that the void is attested by our daily experience. That is why *his* theory of the void, and not that of the Arabian theologians, forms a real contribution to the history of philosophy. Sometimes negative, destructive reasoning is more important than positive reasoning. To destroy the enemy is to win the battle. We should also mention in this connexion

[108] *Ibid.*, p. 14 b.

Crescas's discarding the Aristotelian notion that different elements strive for different places, that fire and air naturally tend upwards. Crescas reduced this variety of forces to one force of gravitation. All bodies are attracted downwards, only air being light is *pressed* upward by some heavier matter. 'Light' and 'heavy' are not different in quality, as Aristotle meant, but different in degree, the degree of attraction that the earth exercises from them.[109] This unification and centralization of forces rids us altogether of the Aristotelian illusion of different 'affinities' and 'natural places', notions which play a considerable part in the problem of place versus space. Thus these two theories of Crescas, the defence of the void and the unification of forces, are landmarks in the progress of Jewish thought.

Coming to Isaac Abrabanel, we are not a little disappointed. Instead of continuing with the development of the pure space problem along the lines of Crescas, he goes back to Aristotelianism. This does not mean that he did not read the *Light of God*. He not only read it, but was even so much infatuated with some parts of it that he incorporated them into his works and forgot to label their real authorship. Compare for example *Light of God*, p. 70, and Abrabanel's *Works of God*, IV, 3. But the plagiarist is not always the disciple. He thus returns to the old-time definition of space as 'the surrounding equal and separate surface'.[110] He adopts the view of Averroes that space came into being with the creation of the material world,[111] that is to say, that there was no pre-existent empty space. He thus answers the question why God created matter in

---

[109] *Ibid.*, p. 9 a.
[110] מפעלות אלהים, IV, 3. See above, note 87.
[111] *Ibid.*, II, 1.

this part of the void rather than another,—there was no pre-existent void altogether; and he cites a similar view of St. Thomas, 'sage of the sages of the Gentiles'.[112] The reader will readily see the eclectic nature of his standpoint. Yet there is one passage in his work which deserves being quoted at length, serving as a fit conclusion to this chapter. It deals with the problem why the mind cannot think of finite space, of limits to extensity, why even in our speaking of an end to the dimensionality of the universe, we seem to imply a 'beyond'. We have seen that Gersonides held this difficulty to be purely linguistic. Crescas on the other hand cited this as a proof for the infinity of space, just as Kant inferred from it that space is a necessity of thought. Abrabanel takes a view similar to that of Gersonides, but there is a strong note of modernity in his explanation. 'It is impossible', he says, 'to conceive the beginning of time without a pre-existent time. Also the limitation of the material world is inconceivable without a beyond-existing place. But this difficulty of conceiving temporal or spatial finitude is purely mental, and does not disprove real finitude. It is in like manner hard to conceive of a thing coming into actual existence without thinking of a preceding potentiality; yet of course it does not mean that there was *actually* a pre-existent potentiality, but only an intellectual idea of such a potentiality. All this is a result of the fact that the phenomena perceived by our senses always have things beyond them in space and things before them in time, and that before these phenomena are actual they are potential; so that these relations of " before " and " beyond ", always present in our perception of things, have impressed themselves on our minds so deeply as to

[112] *Ibid.*, VI, 3.

be unable to conceive of things without those relations. But after a certain amount of reflexion the mind can correct this error arising from perception, and can rid itself of its acquired *habit*, and come to realize that reality is not absolutely conditioned by those relations.'[113]

This is how Abrabanel seeks to explain why space is seemingly a necessity of thought, so that the mind is unable to conceive bounds to the space of the universe. It arises from a 'habit' which the human mind contracted from its perceptual experience to seek a beyond for all things. Yet it takes only a certain amount of mental energy by way of reflexion to transcend this genetically acquired habit, and conceive of an absolute finitude of space. It is not a *necessity* of thought, but a *habit* of thought; and it is the business of a philosophical mind to shake it off.

But this leads us directly to our next problem concerning the infinity of space; and as the contents of this chapter do not require any recapitulation, we will pass on.

[113] *Ibid.*, IV, 3.

CHAPTER III

Infinite Space

ONE of the problems that have troubled the human mind is the problem of space; and one of the aspects of space that have troubled the human mind most, is its infinity. From the philosopher of Stagira to the philosopher of Königsberg, the subject of the infinity of space did not cease to defy and baffle human ingenuity. Our present-day thinkers are mostly silent on this topic. They dread the contest, but they have not overcome it. It still lies like an invincible brute ready to enter the arena. Such being the case, it would be simply preposterous to claim that Jewish philosophy may boast of having solved altogether this overwhelming difficulty, but I do claim that in the course of the progress of Jewish thought some suggestions were made that might lead to a new and better understanding of the problem; and to understand it would be half way to its complete solution.

Let us first turn to Aristotle, who may always serve as a text in any discourse on mediaeval philosophy. His ideas about infinity which are found in the third book of the Physics, and in the tenth of the Metaphysics, are briefly thus. On the one hand we find that infinity is undeniable.

Time is unbegotten and indestructible. We cannot conceive of a moment of time, a Now which is an absolute beginning of a series of duration. Every Now *looks* on one side to a past and on the other to a future: it has a before and after.[114] On the surface it may seem strange that a similar argument could not be advanced to prove the infinity of space: every Here is on one side in touch with a before, and on the other with a beyond. But the argument is really a deeper one. It is repugnant to the entire Aristotelian standpoint of causation, the denial of miraculous creationism, to assume a Now which was not caused by a previous one. Time which marks the duration of the beginningless and endless development of things must in itself be infinite. On the other hand, there must be a limit to material existence. Matter is limited by superficies, and hence finite; and to speak of an infinite number of material bodies is also absurd, for a number is that which can be counted, and hence likewise finite. Besides, an infinite body would be either simple or composite. It could not be, however, a simple body, similar to the one assumed by the earlier physicists, for then it would have consumed by its infinite power all other finite elements, and would have created all things single-handed; but such a monistic theory is contradicted by the fundamental phenomenon of change which implies the existence of contraries in the universe. Nor could that infinite body be a composite without being either a finite number of infinites or an infinite number of finitudes, either alternatives being impossible. Thus after a series of arguments Aristotle concludes the finitude of spatial existence. How then is it—the question is—that infinity seems to be real in time but unreal in space?

[114] Comp. *Or Adonai*, p. 62 a; also מפעלות אלהים, V, 3.

An explanation for this antinomy Aristotle finds in the nature of the concept. It is in accord with his general dynamic standpoint. Infinity denotes duration rather than simultaneity, succession rather than co-extension. Infinity never *is*, but is perpetually becoming. Hence time can be represented as endless, for it is a succession of fleeting moments, each one vanishing and making room for another. But when you seek to attain the infinite by means of a synthesis of spatial parts, you are aiming not at an endless *process of becoming*, but at an endless *state of being* which is not postulated by the true notion of the infinite. The unlimited is not actual but potential, meaning by the latter term not the potentiality of the brass that can become an accomplished fact in the form of the statue, but a peculiar potentiality like that of time, which though actual only in an insignificant and vanishing moment, constantly unfolds itself in a never-ending succession of decay and regeneration. It is a *process*, not a *state*. The usual meaning of the infinite, says Aristotle, is that beyond which there is nothing, but the true meaning is that which always has something beyond.

This analysis of infinity is extremely suggestive. It might be shown what a host of perplexing difficulties would vanish in this new light, as we shall see in the sequel. But it is unfortunate that Aristotle himself did not fully realize the immense fruitfulness of its suggestiveness. He seemingly forgets very soon this well-defined position, namely, that things are always and everywhere finite, but reveal the infinite in the process of change and duration, just as in the arithmetical convergent series every term is limited and gives us a limited quantity when added up with the preceding terms, but there is the infinity of progression, a possibility of enlarging the number of one unit to all eternities. For with this distinction between state and process clearly in his consciousness, how could he possibly speak of a realizable infinitesimal by means of division? My impression is that Aristotle fell a victim to his terminology, to his use of 'potentiality', which always implies something actual, to express his notion of infinity,— an expression which, as he himself felt, hardly suits the meaning. The whole distinction between infinite divisibility and infinite augmentation, the former being affirmed and the latter denied, is unintelligible: *practically* no one would believe that we may divide an object *ad infinitum*, and *theoretically*, even the celestial firmament can form no limit to our augmentation. In the history of the Jewish conception of infinity, this latter potential notion was at first dominating until the former progressive notion was taken up and modified by Gersonides. Let us follow closely this meandering path of the idea of infinity through Jewish philosophy.

Beginning with Saadya, we find that the material universe is held to be limited, having a terrestrial centre and a celestial circumference.[115] This finitude of matter means also the finitude of space, for, as we have seen, the void was not posited by the earlier Jewish thinkers. Saadya pays more attention to the theory of temporal infinity maintained by Aristotle, the refutation of which theory, though somewhat beyond the pale of this work, is nevertheless relevant because of its application to spatial infinity. It is ridiculous, he holds, to say that time had no beginning, for then an infinite number of points have already elapsed;

[115] *Emunot*, I, p. 56: שהשמים והארץ כיון שהתברר שיש להם תכלית
בהיות הארץ באמצע וסבוב השמים סביבותיהם.

in other words, this present moment would be the final term of an infinite series, but an infinite series is that which cannot be completed.[116] Moreover, every passing day is added to the past, and detracted from the future, but anything that has room for an increment, that can be turned into a greater magnitude, is by no means infinite.[117] Furthermore, time is the measure of the spherical movements; and if the former is conceived to be beginningless, the latter must also have a claim to eternity. But those spherical movements are not uniform, there is a variety of ratios between them, while one sphere makes one revolution, another sphere may make three hundred and fifty-five revolutions. If the eternity hypothesis is correct, both spheres have made an infinite number of revolutions, yet sphere B must have certainly made 355 times as many revolutions as those of sphere A. Consequently one infinity would be greater than another infinity, which is absurd, because the infinite is greater than the greatest conceivable quantity.[118] Hence temporal infinity is an impossibility. These arguments, it should be noted, are mentioned by Halevi[119] among the proofs of the Mutakallimun for the theory of creation.

[116] *Ibid.*, I, 59: וכאשר מצאתי עצמי נמצא ידעתי כי ההויה עברה ... על הזמן עד שהגיעה אלי ולולי שיש לי זמן תכלית לא היתה ההויה עוברת בה. See Guttmann's *Die Religionsphilosophie des Saadia*, p. 40, note 3.

[117] *Ibid.*, Part I, p. 74: והוא שכל יום חולף מהזמן לגלגל הוא תוספת על מה שחלף וחסרון מן העתיד ומה שהוא סובל התוספת והחסרון יש תכלית לכחו ותכלית מחיבת החידוש.

[118] *Ibid.*: וכאשר ראינו תנועות השמים מתחלפות עד שקצתם נערכים על קצת על שלשים כפל ועל שלש מאות וחמשים וחמש ועל יותר מזה ידענו שכל אחד מהם יש לו תכלית.

[119] See *Cosari*, Part V, ch. 18, First Axiom.

Baḥya has the following to say about the infinite. He admits that number is infinite. There seems to be no end to the possibility of counting,[120] but actually everything is finite. Imagine a line AB drawn out *ad infinitum*, and take off a definite part AC

```
A      C                          B
───────────────────────────────────
```

Now BC cannot be finite, for two finite lines make no infinite. But AB is of course greater than CB. Thus one infinite would exceed another infinite, which is absurd. Moreover, the very possibility of a part implies that the whole line must be finite, for a part bears a definite ratio to the whole, and is the unit of measurement. Indeed, the extensity of an object is that property of it by virtue of which it can be measured by a part. But the part can bear no ratio to the infinite. Consequently there can be no infinite extensity.[121]

After Baḥya, a full century elapses, marking a blank in the history of the infinite, except perhaps for Gabirol's remarks that infinite, spatial or temporal, is due to formlessness, for that which has form must also be well defined in its limits—a purely Aristotelian position identifying the infinite with the indefinite.[122] At last we come to Abraham

[120] See שער היחוד וחובות הלבבות ch. 8 : אין תכלית למנין; also ch. 5 : ואם נעלה במחשבתנו דבר שאין לו תכלית בפועל ונפריש ממנו קצתו יהיה השאר פחות ממה שהיה קודם מבלי ספק ואם יהיה השאר מאין תכלית יהיה דבר שאין לה תכלית גדול מדבר שאין לו תכלית והוא מה שא״א. This argument is mentioned in Spinoza's *Ethics*. See his note to Part I, prop. xv.

[121] *Ibid.*, ch. 5 : מן הידוע כי כל מה שיש לו חלק יש לו כל כי אין הכל כ״א כלל חלקיו ולא יתכן להיות חלק למה שאין לו תכלית.

[122] *Fons Vitae*, IV, 6, p. 224 'Res autem non est finita nisi per suam formam quia res quae infinita est non habet formam qua fiat unum et differat ab alia ; et ideo essentia aeterna est infinita quae non habet formam.' Comp. V, 23, p. 300, and 29, p. 309.

Ibn Daud, who reiterates the Aristotelian position that only number, which has a potential existence, is infinite, but all actual things are finite. This thesis rests on the following four arguments, all except the first one being Aristotelian.

1. Let two lines AB and CD be drawn *ad infinitum*.

$$\begin{array}{ll} A B \\ \hline C E D \\ \hline \end{array}$$

On CD mark off a finite segment CE. Let the line ED be superposed on AB so that point E coincides with point A. Now the question is, is ED equal to AB? If ED equals AB, it will also equal CD, but how can a part be equal to the whole? If ED is less than AB, how can one infinity be smaller than another? And if ED is not infinite, how does ED plus CE, two finite lines, make an infinite line? This argument resembles Bahya's argument with one line.

2. There can be no infinite number of things, for a number is that which has been counted over, but infinity is that which cannot be counted over. Consequently an infinite number is a contradiction. Besides, a series has at least one limit, but in a beginningless and endless series all terms are intermediary. Consequently an absolutely infinite series is inconceivable.

3. An infinite body would not be in place, for that implies a containing body, and hence a larger magnitude than itself. But what is larger than the infinite? Here the reader may object that from the Aristotelian standpoint not all things are in space. The all-containing sphere is itself not contained.

4. An infinite body would not be at rest, for a body is

only at rest in its 'natural place', which an infinite body does not have. Nor would it be in motion, for a moving body leaves one place and occupies another place which it has not before occupied. But no place is free from the infinite. Hence an unlimited body is impossible.[123]

A critical survey of these four arguments brings out a very important point. We find that the fourth argument is based on an absurd fiction of 'natural places'. The objection to the third has been given. It is the second argument that is truly valid, and defeats the first argument. It points out the absurdity of believing in a numerical or spatial quantity that is infinite. If quantity means anything at all, it is a well-defined relationship between the whole and a supposed part. The only difference between numerical and spatial quantity is that the one denotes a discrete nature and the other a continuous one. But whether it is ten discrete units or ten continuous inches, the relationship between the whole and the part is limited, nothing more and nothing less. Infinity, however, is that which has no limit, and hence cannot enter such relationship at all. Therefore an infinite quantity means nothing else than an infinite finitude, which is utterly meaningless. But if this is true, the fallacy of the first argument of Ibn Daud, and with it many more arguments that may possibly be fashioned after this model, becomes quite evident. If infinity has no quantitative relationships, of course nothing can be added to it or detracted from it—which means a change in those relationships; and the non-existence of infinity cannot be proved on that account. This point was noticed by Maimonides, and amplified by Moses Narboni.

[123] *Emunah Ramah*, pp. 15 ff.

In his exposition of the Kalam [124] Maimonides refers to some of the arguments adduced by that school against the infinite. Now Maimonides himself as an adherent of the Ptolemaic system of astronomy, and the creationistic theory, and as an opponent of the belief in a void, of course maintains absolute finitude in space as well as in time. Only he finds fault with the particular arguments on the basis of which the Mutakallimun negate infinity. They argue that if the world had no beginning in time, there would have elapsed up to this moment an infinite number of points and an infinite number of spherical revolutions and an infinite number of transient accidents. This whole process of fleeting moments and revolving spheres and transitory accidents still goes on, and a thousand years from to-day these infinites will be swelled by a certain number, and the infinity then will be greater than an infinite to-day.[125] Furthermore, if the eternity of the world is true, every celestial body has had an infinite number of revolutions. Now there is a definite ratio between these revolutions. While the terrestrial globe completes its circuit once a year, the lunar globe completes its circuit twelve times in a year. It makes no difference how long you allow these two spheres to revolve, the ratio will always remain 12 : 1. Now allow them to revolve *ad infinitum*, the numbers of their revolutions will be infinite ; but one infinity will be twelve times

---

[124] *Guide*, I, 74, seventh argument; comp. *Cosari*, V, ch. 18, First Axiom.

[125] See also *Eṣ Ḥayyim*, ch. X: שאם לא כן ימצא דבר שאין תכלית לו יותר ממה שאין תכלית לו בשעור שנחסרו להויות באלף שנים בבא זה שאי אפשר. See also *Milḥamot*, p. 343: אחר סור זה ולדבר האחר נוספו שיהיה הזמן החולף בלתי בעל תכלית שאם היה אפשר זה לא יהיה רושם במה שיתחדש מהתנועה בהוספת הזמן . . .

as much as the other, because the ratio subsisting between parts is also the ratio between their totalities, consequently infinity is impossible.[126] A more modern illustration than that of heavenly bodies may be found in dollars and cents. A dollar is to a cent as a hundred to one—a ratio which holds good for any number of these two coins; so that an infinite number of dollars will be a hundred times as much as an infinite of cents. You may invent many more such arguments from any system of weights and measurements, and you will get the same conclusion, contradicting the fundamental notion of the infinite, namely, that it is that greater than which is impossible.

But if we keep our previous conclusions clearly in mind, that the infinite, existent or non-existent, is no quantity, that it can enter into no quantitative relationships, it becomes evident first of all that a thousand years from to-day we will have no greater infinite, whether of temporal moments or spherical revolutions, than now; for the terms 'greater' and 'less' imply a quantitative whole, which infinity is not. And, secondly, it becomes evident that the ratio subsisting between parts falls off as soon as you enter the realm of the infinite, because the ratio is a quantitative relationship, and furthermore because the ratio between parts which is to hold good between their respective totalities is by no means similarly applicable to the infinite, which is not a quantitative totality. Thus as soon as you subject the infinite to mathematical calculations it slips as it were from your grasp, and what you are really dealing with is some big imaginary *finite* magnitude; but then, after you have drawn your conclusion, you exclaim

[126] Gersonides adduces the same argument in his *Milḥamot*, p. 342. Similarly, see Spinoza, *l. c.*

triumphantly 'Eureka'. Maimonides therefore remarks very truly: 'The individual accidents that have passed into non-existence are counted and represented as though they were still in existence, and *as though they were things with a definite beginning; this imaginary number is then either increased or reduced.*' For it is evident that when you wish to add or detract you deal with a totality, and, as Aristotle remarked, the total and the infinite are mutually contradictory. The total is that beyond which there is nothing, and the infinite is that which admits of no beyond altogether. Infinite means endless, a being that is everywhere and whose existence, being immeasurable, cannot be expressed in any mathematical formula, and cannot be the basis of any mathematical equation.[127]

The next man who grappled with this problem was Gersonides. I cannot allow myself, however, to omit two casual but characteristic remarks of two men living before him, Isaac Ibn Latif and Isaac Israeli. The former maintains[128] that the fact that our perception gives us the finite only, is not because reality is finite, but because our perceptive organs are unable to see the infinite.

---

[127] See Narboni, who expatiates on this idea which Maimonides puts very briefly and suggestively.

[128] חכמת המנין מציאותה מורגשת אלא שנמתחת : section 63, רב פעלים והולכת עד לאין תכלית וכן חכמת השיעור הנקראת בלשון ערבי הנדסה גם היא מורגשת ונמתחת והולכת עד שנעלמת מן העין והנשאר מצאותה בשכל בלבד כדמיון מהלך שאין לה תכלית וכמציאות שני קוים שיש ביניהם בתחילת יציאתם שום מרחק על מה שיתרחקו ותחסר המרחק ויתקרבו האחד אל האחד ולא יתכן שיפגשו לעולם ואפילו יצאו לאין תכלית . . . ונמצא החסרון בההרגש לא במורגש. This last illustration Ibn Latif copied literally from the *Guide*, I, 73, prop. 10, where it is quoted from a certain *Book of Cones*, concerning which see Steinschneider, *Heb. Ueber.*, p. 169. It is also cited in the *Or Adonai*, p. 16 a.

That is why our mind does posit an infinite. Israeli, on the other hand, suggests [129] that though the human mind is capable of drawing the line and the surface and the solid *ad infinitum*, reality consists of finite and definitely-shaped objects. The former, Isaac Ibn Latif, was a Kabbalist, moving in a mysterious boundless atmosphere; the latter, Isaac Israeli, was a scientist busying himself with geometrical figures.

The Maimonidean suggestion that infinity does not denote any quantity, served as a starting-point for Gersonides. The latter, first of all, establishes that any quantity, whether numerical or spatial, is by its nature limited. This is a genuine Aristotelian conception. 'But', says Gersonides, 'we do not admit that the reason why matter, number, and magnitude are quantitatively finite is because they are actual, as the Philosopher holds, but because of the intrinsic nature of quantity, the proof of this being that number, even in the case of potential objects like time, must be limited nevertheless.' [130] Thus quantity is by its very definition finite. On the other hand, infinity is beyond any quantitative description. That is why the current definition of infinity as greater than the greatest conceivable body, is radically wrong. The difference between infinite and finite is not merely in *degree* but in *essence*. There is a wide unbridgeable chasm between these two natures. The infinite is irreducible to the finite, nor can the finite be enlarged to the infinite. Divide and subdivide the unlimited, if that is at all possible, and you

---

[129] See *Yesod Olam*, I, 2, p. 5 a: ידוע הוא שהשטח והקו והגוף הוא יוכל להמשך במחשבה אפילו עד אין חקר אבל אין שום אמד מהם נמצא בפועל אלא בעל תכלית ותמונה.

[130] *Milḥamot*, pp. 336 ff.

are still within the realm of the unlimited.[131] On the other hand, even if you were granted eternal life, and were to be engaged all your time in putting together particles of space, you would not step over the boundary of the finite. 'Just as a point will remain a point no matter how much you multiply it, because out of indivisibles you cannot get anything else than the indivisible; so magnitude will always remain magnitude, no matter how much you may multiply it; for *it is infinitely finite with all augmentation.*'[132] The latter is a very pregnant saying: 'Magnitude is infinitely finite.' The infinite is not a product of an inconceivable number of finite spaces. It does not differ from the finite quantitatively, but qualitatively; it is altogether *sui generis.* What that essential quality is, is not quite clearly expressed. But the meaning seems to be this, namely, the removal in our thought of all quantitative determinations and limits. Focus your attention on the spatial fact itself, purely as a simultaneous co-existence without thinking of how far it is spatial, or on time purely as a successive flux, without thinking of the length of its duration; just as you may think of colour without regard to its space limits, and you have the notion of the infinite. Spatial infinity then might be defined as the representation

---

[131] Thus he argues on p. 406, on the basis of this idea which can be expressed in the equation $\frac{\infty}{n} = \infty$, that if we divide infinite time into a finite number of times, we find ourselves in a baffling dilemma. The whole is naturally bigger than the part, but the part of an infinite is likewise infinite, how then can we conceive of two infinites, one greater than the other? Hence time is finite. Comp. also his argument from the 'Lunar Eclipse' on p. 342.

[132] *Ibid.*, 345: כי הוא (i.e. magnitude) תמיד לאין תכלית בעל תכלית עם זאת ההוספה.

of the space-fact itself without regard to its quantitative aspect. This conception of the infinite is novel and interesting; it justifies the possibility of such a notion without involving oneself in numerous antinomies that arise out of a misunderstanding; and the emphasis that it lays on the idea that the infinite is not merely something greater than the greatest conceivable finite, marks an advance in history of the notion. The reader will note that Professor Fullerton recently urged exactly the same point, and on the basis of very much similar arguments.[133]

But conception is one thing, and reality another. Such an abstract idea of the infinite is, like all abstractions, a purely mental fact. In reality, everything is limited and can be represented in a definite quantitative form; and

---

[133] See his *Conception of the Infinite*, ch. 2. I could hardly suspect Professor Fullerton of having read the *Milḥamot*, but there is a very famous thinker in the history of modern philosophy who takes a similar view on the meaning of the infinite, and about whom such a suspicion might be ventured, I mean Baruch Spinoza. In Part I of his *Ethics* he lays down the proposition that substance absolutely infinite is indivisible; and anticipating some difficulty on the part of the reader to grasp the meaning of this paradoxical statement, he seeks to make it comprehensible (see note to prop. xv). But our study of Gersonides makes the meaning clear. The infinite is merely 'the representation of the space-fact itself without regard to its quantitative aspect', and is therefore indivisible. Only a definite quantity can be divided; spatiality as such is found in the same degree in a grain of sand and in the immeasurable ocean. The infinite designates space as a *quality* of matter and consequently suffers no diminution by any process of *quantitative* division. That this indeed is Spinoza's meaning is evident from his definition of eternity which is simply infinity in succession, namely, as 'existence itself in so far as it is conceived necessarily to follow solely from the definition of that which is eternal' and as distinguished from beginningless and endless continuity. Be it also remarked that from this standpoint the distinction between the infinite and the infinitesimal disappears, for the degree of largeness or smallness of matter plays no part in this conception of the infinite.

space is bounded with the bounds of the universe.[134] Yet there is one sense in which infinity can be said to be real, and that is *in process*. There is no end to the mental power of augmentation and diminution. There is no final term to a convergent series enlarging space by a certain unit, nor to a divergent series lessening space by a certain unit. Such a series may go on *ad infinitum*, though every term in that series is but a limited quantity, and gives us a sum total of a limited quantity. All this is because the human mind has acquired the ability to add and detract, and not having experienced anything that refuses addition or subtraction, it can conceive of no limit to that ability. But by addition and subtraction we can get nothing but finite results, so that this mental ability implies two apparently diametrically opposite things, namely, an infinite process with finite results. Indeed, the very exercise of this ability precludes any infinite result, for then the process would come to an end, inasmuch as nothing can be added to the infinite, and thus the process would no more be infinite. Yet the reader will ask, if infinite addition means anything at all, it means that there is no end to the process of adding, consequently there is no end to that which is added. But, as I have shown, if you analyse the term infinite addition, you find that it means that the additional process has no limit beyond which it cannot be carried, but an infinite result which cannot be augmented any more must set up a limit to the process. Hence the inference from infinity of process to infinity of state is

[134] *l. c.*, p. 339. See also p. 386: ובכלל הנה אין כל מה שידמה האדם צודק ולא ידמה האדם כל צודק אבל שם דברים צודקים לא יתכן שידמה אותם האדם כמו כלות העולם אל העדר המוחלט שאינו לא דקות ולא מלוי ומה שידמה לזה.

unjustifiable. That is why 'magnitude is infinitely finite'.

This explanation of Gersonides differs from the theory of potentiality as developed by Aristotle. He cautions [135] the reader not to understand by infinite divisibility or augmentation that a body harbours a possibility to be reduced into an infinitesimal or enlarged into an infinite, because that involves a misunderstanding of the infinite which really cannot be attained by means of the finite. All that is meant is, that a body, being extended, must be divisible; and inasmuch as it is a physical law that a body cannot be destroyed by division, every part must be further divisible. Similarly with augmentation, because any dimensional body has the quality of being enlarged. Thus two series set in, one convergent (1, 2, 3, 4, 5, &c.) and the other divergent (1, $\frac{1}{2}$, $\frac{1}{4}$, $\frac{1}{8}$, $\frac{1}{16}$, &c.). Both series run *ad infinitum*; and it is the condition of such a series, as has been shown, that no infinite term can be reached. Gersonides was more consistent than Aristotle in making no discrimination between infinite divisibility and infinite augmentation.

Thus Gersonides's standpoint makes a genuine contribution to the history of this difficult problem. In completely severing the notion of the infinite from any quantitative relations, and in showing how infinity of process may, and indeed must, go hand in hand with finitude of state, Gersonides may still claim attention from modern thought. We will now pass to the next man, Hasdai Crescas.

The reader perhaps expects from Crescas a defence of the theory of the infinite; the expectation being based on

[135] *Ibid.*, 334.

two reasons: first, Crescas was the first in the history of Jewish thought to challenge Aristotelianism, and thus might have been led to renounce also the Aristotelian theory of the finitude of things; secondly, Crescas was, as we have seen, the first Jewish thinker to postulate pure space outside of and beyond the confines of the universe, thus space at least must be limitless. Well, the reader is not altogether wrong in his expectation, though not quite right. It is true that Crescas took issue with Aristotle on the subject of the infinite, and apparently he explicitly states that space is unlimited. 'It has been explained', he remarks in one place, 'that outside the world there must be either a full or a void, and that boundless dimensionality must exist. And even if it were non-existent, we would have to posit it, just as the geometrician makes use of such a concept in the definition of parallel lines and other fundamental terms.'[136] The latter comparison, however, already casts some suspicion on the author's meaning. The geometrician does not assume the infinite as a necessary fact, but as a hypothetical nature which must conform if real to the general laws and conditions of geometrical figures. It is only in this sense that we say two parallel lines are infinitely equidistant from one another. If now you make further investigation into the author's real opinion, you will find that Crescas at bottom adopted the view-point that was elaborated by Gersonides.

I said that Crescas took issue with Aristotle on the subject of the infinite. Indeed, he attacked all arguments of the Greek philosopher, as well as other arguments that were advanced in negating the idea later by Arabian scholastics. An exposition of this discussion in detail

[136] אור ה׳, p. 16 b.

would really lead me away into the infinite, I mean outside the limits of this work. I shall select two arguments which Shem Tob, the commentator of Maimonides,[137] thinks the most convincing proofs against the existence of the infinite, but which Crescas repudiated. These two arguments are absolutely necessary for our general problem, because they touch the fundamental question whether the mathematical laws of space admit of limitless extension.

The first argument Crescas quotes from Tabrizi,[138] an Arabian commentator of Maimonides, and is called an argument from superposition. Let AB represent a line

$\underline{\quad A \qquad\quad C \qquad\qquad\qquad\qquad B\quad}$

running *ad infinitum*. Mark off a certain distance from A and call it C. Thus we have here two infinite lines AB and CB. Now let the two lines so coincide that C falls on A. Evidently the line CB which is shorter by AC will terminate some distance from AB. Consequently one infinity is greater than another, which is absurd. Hence infinity is impossible. The reader will recall this argument from a Jewish source, namely, from Baḥya, who lived some time before Tabrizi. But it is evident that the author of this proof juggles with the word infinite, and Crescas exposes that fact.

Altogether, Crescas remarks,[139] it is not exact to say

[137] See Shem Tob's Commentary on the *Guide*, II, Introd., prop. 1.

[138] אור ה׳, pp. 5 a and 15 a. The argument is called in Hebrew מופת ההתדבקות. The translation of Tabrizi's Commentary on the twenty-five propositions forming the introduction to Part II, was printed under the title קצת ביאורי מהמורה together with שאלות שאול הכהן. See also Steinschneider, *Heb. Ueber.*, p. 207.

[139] אור ה׳, p. 67 b.: כי באמרנו שהבב״ת אינו גדול מהבב״ת לא נרצה בו שהוא שוה לבב״ת שכבר התבאר שהבב״ת לא יפול שם השוה אבל נרצה בו שאין מדרכו שיתואר הבב״ת בגדול או קטן מבב״ת

that one infinity cannot be greater than another, the fact is that it cannot also equal another. Not only inequality, but also equality, is inapplicable to infinities. For even when we say that a thing equals, we have in our mind a whole quantum, in other words, a limited nature. Hence it is just as absurd to maintain that AB equals, as to maintain that it is greater than CB, for in either case we only *say* that we are dealing with the unlimited; in our mind, however, we have a definite measured amount which we try to compare with another equal or unequal amount. All mathematical considerations, all signs of equality and inequality, must be dropped entirely, if we really wish to conceive the endless. Else we are like the fabulous peacock that sought to escape its feet by flying.

Having this idea clearly in mind, we will find that the whole difficulty with this argument disappears. Let us take an example from time which is supposedly beginningless. Up to now we have a series of moments infinite as to beginning, but limited by this present moment. A day passes by and a number of moments are added to the past. It does not mean, however, that the infinite has been 'increased', for this would suggest that we had a fixed calculable number of moments which we really did not have. We have a case of addition, but we cannot reduce it to a mathematical equation. What are you going to add it to? You are dealing here with unmathematical notions or metamathematical, if you will, and you have no right to

He thus overthrows Gersonides's argument against infinity from the infinite number of lunar eclipses, which not being greater, must be equal to, and coincident with, the infinite number of non-eclipses. According to Crescas one infinity can neither be greater nor equal to another, for it is altogether beyond the category of number. The whole passage is found verbatim in Abrabanel's מפעלות אלהים, IX, 7. See also above, end of ch. 2.

subject them to mathematical treatment. Similarly, you have drawn a line in space from this point *ad infinitum*, a yard further you have drawn a similar line. Both lines represent only an incomplete, so to speak, or unrealized infinite which must be endless as well as beginningless, leading from eternity to eternity. At any rate, all you have is a certain distance which might be added to the infinite line *B*. But to draw hastily a mathematical equation and to seek to get the net result, is to assume an imaginary finite line, or to have a wrong notion of what endlessness means.

The second argument is as follows : [140] If space is infinite we may select any point as a centre through which diameters run *ad infinitum*. The distance between any two diameters which form an angle at the centre becomes wider and wider until the intercepted arc would be infinite. Now the difficulty is twofold. First, if we imagine this infinite space to have a circular movement, how would the moving diameter cross this infinite intercepted arc? An infinity is just that which cannot be crossed over. Secondly, how can the arc be infinite when it is limited by the two diameters? and if it is not limited by them, the diameters must be finite. And if they are finite, the intercepted arc is naturally finite too.

Now, first, Crescas removes the objection from motion. It is inconceivable how an infinite body could move. To move means to leave an occupied place and to occupy an unoccupied place, but no place is free from the infinite. He now turns to the second difficulty. An intercepted arc

---

[140] אור ה׳, pp. 7 a, 16 b. This argument is in the main identical with Tabrizi's 'argument from scales', מופת הסולמי. Cf. *l. c.*, p. 5 b. Comp. also Spinoza's *Ethics*, part I, prop. xv, note.

between two infinite diameters would eventually be infinite. But if it is infinite, how is it limited by the two diameters, and if it is unlimited by them, they must be finite. To this Crescas replies, an infinite line does not mean one that has infinite extent between its ends—a meaning which is of course contradictory and nonsensical. Similarly, it is absurd to look on this diameter for a point which will be an infinite distance from the centre; and inasmuch as the arc could be infinite only at such a point, it is evident that an infinite arc is impossible. What then do we mean by 'the infinite diameter'? Just this, that there is no limit to the possibility of extending the line, because space itself cannot be conceived to have limits; that it can be infinitely prolonged and nevertheless preserve its finite nature. This fact may at first seem strange, but it is no more strange, says Crescas, than the fact cited in the *Book of Cones*,[141] that two lines starting at a distance from one another, and drawing nearer while they go on, never come in contact, even though you may prolong them *ad infinitum*. Infinity then denotes a process which may be perpetually carried on without breaking up the integral nature of the object, just as finitude denotes a limit which a certain process cannot surpass without destroying the peculiar nature of the object, as when we say that a body is only finitely divisible. Thus the diameter is infinite because it can endlessly be extended, though it always preserves its finiteness, though it never reaches a point which is at a boundless distance from the centre, and so never possibly intercepts an infinite arc. The reader will recall the pregnant saying, 'Magnitude is infinitely finite'. The key-note of this whole discussion is that there is an infinite process, which naturally implies finite results.

[141] See above, note 128.

Thus there are two fundamental notions about the infinite which stand out very clearly from these two arguments. The first argument shows that infinity is in nowise reducible to terms of finitude and quantity, and vice versa. Hence the idea that we conceive the infinite by means of a successive synthesis of finites is erroneous. We may delve deep into the bottomless abyss, we may soar on our imagination to the dreary regions of pure space, we may make a life-long, or an eternity-long, successive synthesis, but we will still find ourselves much within the boundaries of the finite, simply because finite plus finite equals finite. It is not by widening limits, but by removing limits, by thinking away all quantitative determinations, that we are allowed a glimpse of the infinite.

The second argument obviates an objection from the reader, namely, if space can be endlessly enlarged, it must finally be endlessly large. The word 'finally' is not appropriate. Infinity denotes a process which is endless, consequently it has no final term. Hence there can be no infinite state or infinite result, because that would be a final term. The second argument then brings out the complementary idea that there is a logical harmony between infinity of process and finitude of results.

Thus we have seen how this conception as a whole was first faintly suggested by Maimonides, given prominence by Narboni, elaborated and crystallized by Gersonides, and finally clarified by Hasdai Crescas. It may, therefore, be justly called the view of infinity of mediaeval Jewish philosophy—a view that may claim even at the present day the serious attention of the student who is perplexed by the tangle of numerous contradictions and antinomies which this problem presents.

Conclusion

A brief *résumé* of the chief points in the preceding discussion is now in order. I shall select the four central problems that have occupied our attention so far, and examine the solution offered by the mediaeval Jewish thinkers. These problems are: (1) the reality of empirical space, (2) the infinite divisibility of space, (3) the existence of absolute space, and (4) the infinity of space.

(1) In Jewish philosophy space is conceived as an objective reality. By 'reality' I understand the existence of a thing in the objective world independent of our perception. The mediaeval mind in general saw no problem in the reality of space. One might have disputed on how many angels could stand tip-toe on a pin-head, but that the pin-head exists with a certain magnitude of extension, no one entertained any doubt. It is only the modern mind, hypersophisticated, philosophically gone astray, that nervously asks whether this vast extension above and below and around us is not a mere illusion. Not only did the Jewish thinkers affirm the independent existence of space, but some even went so far as to take a geometric view of things and conceive the corporeal essence in terms of space. Matter, they maintained, is not merely that which takes up space, but it *is* space. All other characteristics that a certain object may possess are altogether unimportant for a pure conception of matter. A material object, according to these thinkers, may be defined as a limited magnitude of space that possesses certain qualities. Thus space and matter are synonymous terms. Other thinkers are less radical, and put space in the category of qualities. Corporeality means for them some mysterious substrate,

the conception of which requires no space determinatives. Yet in reality, all admit, space is inseparable from matter.

(2) But if unextended matter is an impossibility, it is evident that the Arabian atomic hypothesis, which reduces matter to ultimate non-magnitudinal parts, must be rejected. A non-magnitudinal part is in the first place impossible in itself, and secondly, how could it produce extension by combining with a similar part? A point is zero of extension, and you may add zeros *ad infinitum* without ever getting a number. Besides, the word 'combine' itself, if it is meant in a physical and not in a chemical sense, which is irrelevant in this connexion, implies a limit coming in contact with another limit, and a limit is a point before which there is a point which is no limit. In short, combination implies that that which combines is an aggregate of points, and consequently extended. Hence the idea that matter is composed of ultimate spaceless parts must be abandoned. The truth is, that no matter how much you may divide and subdivide a piece of matter, you will always get something that is further divisible. Of course, practically, you will eventually reach a *minimum sensibile*; theoretically, however, nothing prevents us from continuing with our process of division. Extension means 'alongsidedness of parts', and hence divisibility. Consequently, as long as you have matter you have divisibility. Therefore anything, however small and minute, can be divided *ad infinitum*. But here a dreadful gap opens up wide before us. If things are infinitely divisible, they must have an infinite number of parts, but how can a finite object contain an infinite number of parts? How can we move over even the smallest distance? And how could Achilles overtake the tortoise when the distance between

them is infinitely divisible, and each half of the distance that Achilles covers leaves another half between them, growing smaller and smaller to be sure, but never becoming zero? Indeed, one might ask how they can both begin to move, since the very first step, even that of the tortoise, involves a crossing of an infinite abyss? The fourth point, on the infinity of space, will give an answer to these questions also.

(3) So much for empirical space, or concrete extensity. This is undeniably real, as real as matter of which it is the distinguishing characteristic. But is there such a thing as pure space, mere dimensionality outside of and beyond the world of matter? Here opinions differed, the majority being against the existence of a void. In accepting the Aristotelian notion of space as 'the inner limit of the containing body', or a mere relation of contiguity between two objects, the Jewish thinkers had to endorse the exclusion of the possibility of pure space. For if by space, as distinguished from concrete extension, is meant merely contiguity, it is evident that where there are no bodies, there can be no space. This is precisely the Leibnizian position. Yet there is this critical remark to be made. Such a position might indeed explain the possibility of conceiving the vanishing of the space order, with the annihilation of the world of matter. But if this relationship of contiguity is to supplant the notion of space, by inheriting also its apodictic certainty; I mean, if the mind necessarily postulates such contiguity in connexion with matter; if an object cannot be conceived to exist outside of such relationship, the question may be asked, how is the universe as a whole conceivable without such relations? What, if pure space is denied, is con-

tiguous with the confines of the world? By what is matter limited? Indeed, such an objection, we have seen, was raised against the Aristotelian theory of the existence of a sphere which is all-containing and not contained. But the Jewish thinkers who negated the void would have flatly refused to confer 'apodictic certainty' on the relationship of contiguity. Some, it is true, were puzzled by the question: What is there beyond? And after they have proved by a series of arguments, to their own satisfaction, that space has limits and there is nothing beyond, they suddenly started at their own expression: Yes, but does not the word 'beyond' suggest a spatial background? The whole puzzle, however, was solved very truly by Abrabanel. The mind constantly receives spatial impressions from the external world, so that it has acquired a habit to consider things in spatial relations. Hence a solitary object that is shorn of these relations, is not easily conceivable, but it is not inconceivable. The human mind can transcend this habit and conceive of a finite totality which stands in no spatial relations with anything else.

(4) And so I come to the last point in our discussion. We saw in connexion with the idea of the void, that the finitude of space is held by the majority of Jewish thinkers. But infinite space presents a problem of its own. On the one hand many mathematical demonstrations might be made showing the impossibility of infinity; on the other hand, infinity seems to be a positive fact of experience. There can be no limit to the possibility of enlarging an object, just as we have seen that there can be no limit to the possibility of dividing a certain object. And if that is so, will not these two antithetical processes evolve two

bodies, one infinitely large, and the other infinitely small? Jewish philosophy has this to say on this serious difficulty. It is contradictory to speak of a body that is 'infinitely large' or 'infinitely small'. The terms 'large' and 'small' denote quantity, they present to our mind a definite *limited* magnitude; and infinity means *limitless*. Infinity, above all, must be absolutely distinguished from quantity; it is just by the removal of quantity that you conceive the infinite. And the fundamental error in the first Kantian antinomy is just this: that infinity is conceived as a successive synthesis of parts, whereas true infinity refuses being measured because it is just the reverse of measure, and excludes the notion of a part because it is indivisible as well as unaugmentable, being no definite magnitude, and is not obtained by a series of successive syntheses, because you may choose the greatest conceivable magnitude and multiply it by the greatest imaginable number, and what you will have will be a finite object as finite as a grain of sand and a blade of grass. Finite plus finite equals finite.

What then does infinity mean? It represents a process that may be carried endlessly without destroying the object; just as finitude represents such a process that will ultimately reach a limit, the crossing of which would spell injury to the object. It is in this sense that we say matter is infinitely augmentable, meaning that we can enlarge and further enlarge a given magnitude of matter *ad infinitum*, without ever producing an infinite magnitude, because that would mean the loss of matter which is by nature limited and circumscribed. Indeed, it is absurd to believe that such an infinite will eventually be reached, because then the process will cease, infinity being unaugmentable, and the process will therefore be finite. Hence an infinite process presupposes finite results, and as one Jewish thinker cleverly remarked: Matter is infinitely finite. Similarly, infinite divisibility denotes that the process of division may be carried on theoretically *ad infinitum*, without bringing about the loss of the object. Yet this endless process never produces the infinitesimal, because that would involve the end of the process. But does not this mean, the reader will ask, that we could resolve a piece of matter into an infinite number of parts? No; first of all an infinite number is a contradiction of terms, and, secondly, if such an infinite number could possibly be attained the process of division would cease, but it is endless. Hence while each part becomes smaller and the number of parts greater, they cannot both overleap the boundaries of the finite. Thus Zeno's puzzles vanish like shadows in the light. We do not move over infinities, and Achilles can easily overtake the tortoise. What we have to bear in mind is only this, that infinity is a process, not a state.

Thus I have outlined briefly the Jewish standpoint in the problem of space, and I might conclude here perfectly well. Yet I should like to discuss one more point with the reader before we part. It is the Jewish empirical view versus the modern doctrine of the subjectivity of space. I fear that many a Kantian reader will leave this volume— if he looks at it at all—with a smile: Objectivity of space, Mediaevalism! Yet I believe that the phenomenalistic theory has hindered rather than helped man in his desire to know his whereabouts, so as to adjust the interrelations in the best possible manner. Kant did not explain things, but transformed the world into a dreadful yawning abyss and called it Noumenon. He argued that we can mentally annihilate and think away matter, but we cannot think away space, consequently space is a necessity of thought. But for myself, I cannot see how we can think away matter. Of course we can stop thinking at all, then we have thought away space, also; but to think and not to think of things is absurd. When we think, of course we think something and about something. Objects of experience are the contents of our thought; think away those objects, and thought becomes meaningless. And as for space being a necessity of the mind, Abrabanel, we have seen, explains it very clearly. It is a habit contracted by the mind under the pressure of constant spatial experience. Had the human mind been born in a spaceless universe, spacelessness would have become a necessity of thought. For what is consciousness if not the manifold impresses of external stimuli? Hence the very idea that space is a necessity of thought proves that it is a necessity of reality. To deny this means to assume that the mind is some independent spiritual nature capable of engendering an order of existence. Of course, the infant undoubtedly has some dim sense of space, but this may have been because of the fact that the universal reality of space has developed in the human mind in the course of its evolution a spatial sense, because it helped the mind to adjust its relations to the external order; and so this innate spatial sense is itself evidence for the reality of space. But I cannot take up this phase of the question here.

Thus I submit this Jewish empirical standpoint to the student of the problem of space, as a possible solution.

GLOSSARY OF SOME HEBREW PHILOSOPHICAL TERMS IN CONNEXION WITH THE SUBJECT OF SPACE

אָנָה one of the categories denoting place 'where'. מאמר האנה הוא בתארך הגוף ביחוסו למקומו שהוא שוכן עליו כאמרך פלוני היושב בבית או בעיר (רוח חן).

גְבוּל. See מקום.

גּוֹדֶל magnitude. גודל נבדל pure, unoccupied magnitude. See *Or Adonai*, p. 4.

גּוּף (Arab. جوف) body. וכל מי שצריך מקום הוא גוף (אשכול הכופר, כ״ח).

גֶרֶם (Arab. جرم) (1) body. Usually applied to the heavenly bodies. יניעו מניעי הגרמים השמימיים (הקד׳ רלב״ג למלחמות). (2) atom, ותו הגרם (העצם הפרדי) בהמצאו יעכב המקום בעצמו וימנע חברו מבוא במקומו (ערוגת החכמה להראב״ע, כרם חמד, IV).

גֶשֶׁם (Arab. جسم). Ḥarizi in his glossary, prefixed to his translation of the *Guide*, derives it from Isa. 44. 14, וגשם יגדל, which he interprets 'And the bulk he increases'. (1) body. See *Ruaḥ Ḥen*, ch. 1, וגדר הגשם הוא כל דבר שיש לו ג׳ רחקים. Sometimes גושם. See *Sefer Maẓref*, ed. Gollancz, p. 23. It is noteworthy that Ḥarizi invariably renders גֶּסֶם by גוף. המנעות הכנס גשם בגשם impenetrability. See *Or Adonai*, p. 14. (2) atom, שבורא הדברים יש לו גשמים רוחניים קדמוניים מהם ברא אלה הגשמים המורכבים (אמונות ודעות, מ״א, פ״ג).

דְבֵקוּת continuity, extendedness שהנשם מליצה מהדבקות אשר אפשר (as כמה המתדבק. שיונחו בו שלשה שלוחים (מאמר לר׳ יוסף אבן עקנין) distinguished from המתחלק or המתפרק) spatial magnitude. See *Milḥamot*, p. 124, שהחכמה המתדבק מתחלק אל מה שלא יתחלק.

דַק atom. כי גבול הדק זה הוא שלא יחלק לנו (אשכול הכפר, כ״ח).

117

הגרמה penetrability. שאלה מה אמתת הגבול, תשובה הדק שמוגבל
באמתתו מהגרמת דבר אחר הוא יקרא גבול (אשכל הכפר, סה).

התדבקות continuity, extendedness. ... שההתדבקות היא צורת הגשם
וזה שהסתלקות התדבקות יפסיד עצמות אותו הגשם (אמונה רמה, I, 2).

התפשטות dimension. עצם שיש לו מן העובי והמקשיות מה שבהם
אפשר שיונחו בו ג' התפשטיות (אמונה רמה, שם).

חלל (Arab. حلل) pure space. שלא היה דבר קודם יצירת העולם
ולא חלל להאמר כי הוא ריקן ולא להאמר כי היא מלא (פירוש ר״י
הברצלוני לס׳ יצירה, 149).

חללות space-interval. הרוחק אשר בין תכליות המקיף והוא אשר
יקרא חללות (אור ה׳, 5). Comp. Aristotle's *Physics*, iv. 211 b 7
διάστημά τι τὸ μεταξὺ τῶν ἐσχάτων.

חלק atom. הדבר שלא יחלק ויחתך לשנים הוא יקרא חתיכה או חלק
ולא יתכן קאלוא מן יוגד גסם (אשכל הכפר, ס״ה). See *Guide*, I, 51,
בונה ch. 73 Also. ויברהן עלי אבטאל אלוג׳ למא אֻתֿבת וג׳ודה
אלא מרכّבא מן הדֿה אלאג׳זא אלמתמאתֿלה ... כמה כאן יעתקד
אפיקורס וגירה מאן קאל באלוג׳. Comp. Fanari in Igi's *Almawakif*,
Cairo, 1907, 43, جسم مركَّب من اجزاء متشابهة. Ibn Tibbon,
however, has for جزء the expression חלק מתחלק שאינו. Comp.
Saadya, *Amanat*, 36, وان بعض النظَّارين التجأ الى قول بجزء لا يتجزَّأ.
This last expression is a faithful rendering of the original Greek
terms ἄτομον and σώματα ἀδιαίρετα. Curiously enough Ḥarizi
renders ניו in ch. 51 by השדים, well deserving Narboni's remark
מי שכנהו על השד אחוזו השד.

חתיכה Karaitic term for atom. וזהו הדק שקוראים אותו חכמינו
חלק. See חתיכה (עץ חיים, פ״ד).

מילוי occupied space, 'full', Gr. πλέον. אם אין שם גשם הנה אין
מלא. Adj. שם מילוי (אור ה׳, 14).

מצב one of the nine categories, properly designating the relative
position of the parts of the body, see *Ruaḥ Ḥen*. Often identical
with אנה denoting place 'where', והוא היוצא מן האפס שאינו נוצל
מן מקרה המצב (עץ חיים, פ״ד).

מקום (1) space, extensity. שהמקום האמתי לדבר הוא רוחק אשר
בין תכליות המקיף (אור ה׳, 15). (2) In the Aristotelian sense, as
a containing body. מקום הוא השטח הפנימיי מהגרם המקיף הממשש

לשטח המקומם (ספר גדרים למנחם בונאפוס). Thus it corresponds to both τόπος and χώρα. מקום כולל, מקום מיוחד corresponds to the Aristotelian distinction between accidental and essential place; see Aristotle's *Physics*, iv. 211 a. וזה כי לכל דבר נשמי יש שני מקומות מקום כולל ומקום מיוחד המשל ראובן יושב בזה הבית הוא מקום כולל ואמנם נמצא במקום מיוחד ממנו שגדרו הוא תכלית הגשם המקיף במתקומם הנוגע בו (מנחת קנאות לר' יחיאל מפיסא, צד, 26 (Berlin, 1898, Ed. Kaufmann. (3) Position, direction, Ger. *Gegend*. Thus Ḥarizi in *Moreh*, I, 4, has כי העינים לא ישינו אלא נוף ובמקום וקצת מקריו, for which the original reads אך לא תדרך אלאעין אלא גסמא ופי נהה ובעץ אעראצה. The meaning of this passage is not made clear by Scheyer (see his note *a.l.*), nor by Munk, who renders ופי נהה by 'd'un certain côté': Maimonides here refers to the Mutazilite theory that sight can only be caused by an object occupying a certain position (جهة) relative to the seer, but as the Deity is beyond space relation to any object, it can never have a visual sensation, a theory much disputed by the Asherites. See M. J. Müller's translation of *Ibn Rushd's Philosophie u. Theologie*, pp. 70, 71. (4) יטריד מקום occupies space conveying the sense of impenetrability, הרחקים אם לא היו בעלי חומר לא יטרידו מקום .... הנה יצדק מורכב שהרחקים בעלי חומר יטרידו המקום אשר מזה הצד הוא נמנע הכנס גשם בגשם (אור ה', יד). The meaning therefore of the very difficult passage in *Moreh*, I, 51, העצם הפרדי אינו במקום אבל יטריד הגבול (others read יטריח המחוז), is that though an atom is in itself unextended, it still controls certain space-limits within which no other atom can penetrate. Munk's interpretation of the passage (see *a. l.*) hardly seems to me justifiable. He reads into it a certain Leibnizian theory that the atom, like the mathematical point, occupies an atom of space only, an interpretation little substantiated by his own citation from Ġorġani's *Kitab al-Taʿrifat*, which is as follows: المكان عند المتكلمين هو الفراغ المتوهم الذي يشغله للجسم وينفذ فيه ابعاده للحيّز عند المتكلمين هو الفراغ المتوهم الذي يشغله شى ممتدّ كالجسم او غير ممتدّ كالجوهر الفرد, i.e. the term 'makanun' is ascribed only to such an object which occupies a certain space and also permeates it with its own dimensions, while 'ḥayyazun' is ascribed to objects, both extended and unextended, which only occupy it but do not completely fill it with their voluminousness. If now حيّز were an atom of space, it could not be ascribed to a شى ممتدّ. Our interpretation is furthermore corroborated by Hadassi's definition of the term גבול, viz. הדק המונבל באמתתו מהגרמת דבר אחר הוא יקרא גבול המונבל בעיניך (עץ חיים, ס״ה). So Ibn Rushd, in commenting on the term جهة, writes in the first part of his *Masail*: وكذالك نريد هولنا كائن فى جهة أنّه لو وُجد جوهر اخر لكان لا يجوز أن يحصل بحث هر وأدّما يكون عن يمينه أو يساره .... Lastly, Ibn Ezra, who takes the standpoint of the Mutakallimun, remarks ותו הנרם בהמצאו יעכב מקום בעצמו וימנע חברו מבוא במקומו .... והנגרמים בהאספם גוף קראוהו החכמים בדעתם, ותו הגוף שיש לו אורך ורוחב ועומק, וכו' (ערוגת החכמה), where the meaning is clear; i.e. every spatial body is composed of atoms, each one unspatial by itself yet controlling certain space-limits within which no other atom can penetrate, so that the extensity of a body is due to the empty spaces between the spaceless atoms. Other Hebrew expressions used for the Arabic يشغل للحيّز are ימלא מקום (see עולם קטן, p. 15) יתפוש מקום (q. v.) יעסק מקום (ערוגת החכמה) יעכב מקום (see quotation from ספר נעימות in Schreiner's *Kalam*, p. 37).

מרחק (1) distance. אפשרות התקצר המרחק לבלתי תכלית (אור ה׳, ט״ז). (2) dimension. שהמנע גשם בגשם הכנסו הוא מצד מרחקיו הג׳ בלבד (שם), identical with רחק, q. v.

מתוסף augmentable. מתוסף אל מתוסף infinitely augmentable. ואם היה שיתוסף זה המספר אל מה שיתוסף (מלחמות ה׳, 334).

מתחלק divisible. מתחלק אל מתחלק infinitely divisible. וזה הדבר יחויב שימצא בזמן במה שהוא זמן רוצה לומר שהוא יתחלק אל מה מתחלק אל מה שלא יתחלק. שיתחלק (מלחמות ה׳, 334) finitely divisible.

מתקומם a thing in space, contained. שאין מקום מבלי מתקומם (עולם קטן, 15).

GLOSSARY 121

נקודה (1) point. See definition in חבור המשיחה והתשבורת by Abraham bar Ḥiyya, Berlin, 1912, where a number of geometrical terms are defined. (2) נקודות קטנות atoms. שהוא קבץ מהם נקודות קטנות והם החלקים אשר לא יחלקו (אמונות, מ״א, פ״ג).

עוסק occupies space. ומחויב הדק שהוא עוסק במקום מונע זולתו מהיותו במקום שלו (עץ חיים, פ״ב).

עסוק במקים the act of occupying space. ואשור הדק הוא עסוקו במקום. Sometimes עסוק alone. מקום שם משותף עניגו (שם). הראשון לעסוק הגוף (שם, XX).

עצם (prop. substance) (1) atom. כי כל נשם מורכב על דעת אנשי עצם פרדי (2). שקול הדעת מעצמים רבים (ספר צחות לראב״ע). See الجوهر المنفرد (Arab. الجوهر الفرد), not to be confused with الجوهر المنفرد, Ibn Rushd's *Kitab al-Masail*, part I) atom, corresponding to Joannes Philoponus's μέριχα οὐσία (cf. Schreiner's *Kalam*, pp. 9, 45, note 2, and Munk, *Guide*, I, 186) שהעצם הפרדי מציאותו במקרים ההם ולא ימלט מהם (מו״נ, ח״א, ע״נ).

פאה (prop. side, limit, Arab. جهة) Karaitic term for relative space. See *Eẓ Ḥayyim*, ch. 4, ועת צאת הדק מן האפס והסגל (comp. Falaquera's *Moreh ha-Moreh*, Presburg, 1837, p. 62, במקום בתחלת. (דרך חמישי והוא דרך הסגול...א״כ הסגול בתבנית חדושו לא יתואר לא שוכן ולא מתנועע שהשוכן הוא שישרת ב׳ עתות במקום אחד ותחלת החדוש אינו שהות שתי עתות והמתנועע שהמתנועע יתחדש אחר מכחישו וקראוהו בשם חניה למען ההויה ההיא הוסגל בפאה זולת פאה. It is probably in this sense that Hadasi uses the term in *Eshkol Hakofer*, ch. 29, כי הנראה לעין הוא מה שיכיל במקום או בפאה. See also ch. 28. Comp. *Sefer Ne'imot*, quoted in Schreiner's *Kalam*, p. 37, והחתיכה אשר אם תמצא ותעסק ותתפוש פאה ותקבל האפעים והאפע הוא אשר אם ימצא לא יעסק ולא יתפוש מקום. Ibn Ezra also uses the term in his ערוגת החכמה.

פנאי empty space, void (Gk. κενόν). לפי סברתם האומרים בהימנעות; פנוי; As an adj. נשם בב״ת יש שם בהכרח פנאי (אור ה׳, 15) see *ibid.*, 14 b.

קו an imaginary line composed of mathematical points or of atoms. See *Eẓ Ḥayyim*, ch. 4, and Ibn Rushd's *Masail*, part I.

והם הרוחניים אשר הם מדמים atoms. (الروحانيّات .Arab) **רוחניים**
במחשבתם כאבק וכדק מכל דק ובחלק שאין מתחלק (אמונות מ"א, פ"ג).

רחק (1) interval, stereometric content, the Aristotelian διάστημα.
שהמקום האמתי לדבר הוא הרחק אשר בין תכליות המקיף (אור ה', 15 b);
(2) dimension. רחקים נבדלים = dimensions of pure. והנה
הרחקים הנבדלים ענינם המקום הפנוי לקבל רחקי גשם (שם).

רקות void. ג"כ קדמוני המדברים שהיו עיקר חכמת המדברים מאמינים
שהרקות נמצא (מו"נ, 73 ,I). Ḥarizi uses the word ריקם for a noun.

שטח plane, surface composed of four atoms. Cp. קו.

שלוח dimension. ואחד השלוחים יקרא אורך והאחד רוחב והשלישי
עומק. See Moritz Löwy, *Drei Abhandlungen*, Berlin, 1879,
Heb. sect., p. 11.

תכלית (1) limit, end = סוף; בעל תכלית, finite; בלתי בעל תכלית,
infinite. (2) Limiting surface, superficies. Cp. the current
Aristotelian definition of Makom, תכלית מקיף שוה נבדל.

INDEX

Aaron of Nicomedia, 44, 45, 50, 55, 56, 66.
Abrabanel, Don Isaac, I, 37, 39, 43-5, 66, 67, 70. 85-7, 106, 113, 116.
Abraham bar Ḥiyya, 40, 44, 65.
Absolute Space, 61-7; Aristotelian notion of, 63; the traditional view in Jewish philosophy, 63 *et seq.*; Gabirol, Abraham bar Ḥiyya, Joseph ibn Zaddik, Abraham ibn Daud, Aaron the Karaite and Gersonides on, 65, 66; Crescas challenges the Aristotelian conception of, 66-9; his influence on Albo, 68 *et seq.*; Abrabanel accepts the Aristotelian definition of, 71; summary of, 118.
Abu Hamd, 43.
Achilles, 111, 112, 115.
Acht Bücher Physik, 15.
Albo, Joseph, 55, 66, 68, 70.
Aquinas, Thomas, 86.
Archiv für Geschichte der Philosophie, 30.
Aristotle, 4, 5, 7, 8, 14-21, 23, 27, 33, 36, 37, 39, 45-50, 55, 57, 62-4, 66-72, 77, 85, 88, 91, 93, 94, 98, 99, 103, 104, 112, 113.
Aspects of Rabbinic Theology, 28.
Atomism, *see* Infinite Divisibility.
Attributenlehre, 64.
Averroes, 43, 85.

Baeumker, 33.
Bahya, 93, 94, 105.
Bergson, Henri, 2.
Bibago, Abraham, 44.
Bible, 27, 62.
Book of Cones, 98, 108.
Book of Creation, see *Sefer Yeẓirah*.
Botarel, Moses, 67.
Brothers of Purity, 36.

Cohen, Hermann, 2.
Conception of the Infinite, 101.
Cosari, 27, 28, 49, 52, 78, 92.
Crescas, 41, 63, 66 72, 78-86, 103-5.
Delitzsch, Franz, 44.

Democritus, 47, 49.
Descartes, 20, 25, 28, 34, 35.
Dieterici, 36.
Die Religionsphilosophie des Saadia, 92.
Dogmas, see Ikkarim.
Drei Abhandlungen by Moritz Löwy, 42.

Elijah, del Medigo, 37.
Empirical Space, 22-46; Plato on, 5-14, 33-4; Aristotle on, 33-4; Descartes, 34; Kant, 34-5; Aristotelian conception shared by Saadya, Maimonides, Samuel ibn Tibbon, 36; Elijah del Medigo, Abrabanel, Jehiel of Pisa, 37; pseudo-Platonic conception represented by Isaac Israeli, the elder, 32; Gabirol, 38 *et seq.*; Abraham bar Ḥiyya, 40; Joseph ibn Zaddik, 40; Abraham ibn Daud on, 41; the latter followed by Joseph ibn Aknin, 43; Moses Narboni, Shem Tob ben Shem Tob and others share the pseudo-Platonic view on, 44 *et seq.*; Abrabanel on, 45; summary of, 110.
Emunah Ramah, 42, 66, 95.
Emunot we-Deot, 22, 24, 36, 50, 52, 62, 91.
Epistolae ad P. des Bosses, 55.
Eshkol Hakofer, 45, 49.
Eṣ Ḥayyim, 44, 50, 55, 56, 66, 96.
Ethics, 93, 101, 107.
Euclidean, 69.

Festschrift, Steinschneider's, 27.
Fons Vitae, 26, 38, 39, 53, 54, 65, 96; see *Meḳor Ḥayyim*.
Fullerton, 101.

Gabirol, 26, 27, 31, 36, 38-90, 93, 96, 98 *et seq.*
Galen, 27.
Gersonides, 57-60, 65, 66, 75-8, 80, 86, 91, 97-9, 101, 102, 104, 106, 109.
Geschichte der alten Philosophie, 7.

Greek Philosophy to the time of Socrates, 7.
Grundriss einer systematischen Theologie des Judentums, 24.
Guide for the Perplexed, 55, 56, 61, 72, 96, 98.
Guttmann, 39, 93.

Hadassi, Judah, 45.
Hakarmel, 27.
Hebräische Uebersetzungen, 67, 98, 105.
Heraclitus, 12.
Hirschfeld, 27.
Histoire des langues sémitiques, 1.
Hobot ha Lebabot, 40.
Horowitz, Saul, 22, 26, 28.
Husik, Isaac, 39.

Ibn Aknin, Joseph, 27, 42, 44, 45.
Ibn Daud, Abraham, 42, 44, 45, 65, 73, 75.
Ibn Ezra, Abraham, 72.
Ibn Latif, Isaac, 73, 78, 97.
Ibn Rushd, 119, 121.
Ibn Zaddik, Joseph, 28-31, 41, 44, 65, 67, 72, 78.
Iggerot ha-Rambam, 22.
Ikkarim, 56, 66, 68, 73.
Infinite Divisibility, 46-60; Aristotelian doctrine versus Atomism of the Mutakallimun, 47-9; Judah Hadassi as well as other Jewish thinkers, with the exception of ibn Ezra, uphold the Aristotelian theory of, 49; Isaac Israeli the elder on, 49 *et seq.*; Saadya introduces Zeno's paradoxes, 59; Gabirol's arguments in favour of, 53; Maimonides on, 55; Gersonides's solution of Zeno's puzzles, 57 *et seq.*; summary of, 111-18.
Infinite Space, 88-109; Aristotle's theory of, 88; potential versus progressive infinity, the former at first prevalent in Jewish thought, 91; Saadya on, 92; Bahya and Gabirol on, 93; ibn Daud's proofs against, 94-5; Maimonides and Narboni disprove the contention of the Mutakallimun against, 96-8; Isaac ibn Latif and Isaac Israeli on, 98; Gersonides's contribution to the problem of, 98-103; Crescas's criticism of the Aristotelian theory of, 104-9; summary of, 113-15.

Isaac Israeli the Elder, 1, 22, 38, 45, 49, 53.
Isaac Israeli the Younger, 50, 56, 98, 99.

Jehiel b. Samuel of Pisa, 37.
Jowett, 6.
Judah ha-Levi, 28, 91.

Kalam, 37, 49, 56, 71, 96.
Kant, 8, 14, 20, 34-6, 46, 57, 86, 114, 115.
Kaufmann, D., 64.
Kohler, K., 24.

Leibniz, 55, 112.
Leisegang, 2.
Levi b. Gerhon, 56.
Light of God, see *Or Adonai*.
Locke, John, 8.
Löwy, Moritz, 42.

Maimon, Salomon, 74.
Maimonides, 36, 40, 55, 56, 62, 73, 95, 96, 98, 99, 105, 109.
Mekor Hayyim, 27, 39, 65.
Malter, H., 22.
Mélanges, 26.
Metaphysics, 7, 88,
Microcosm, 2, 8, 29, 31, 40, 41, 65, 72, 73.
Mif'alot Elohim, 71, 85, 89, 106.
Milhamot Adonai, 56, 66, 75, 96, 97, 99, 101.
Milhamot, see *Milhamot Adonai*.
Minhat Kenaot, 37, 69.
Monads, 55.
Moreh, see *Guide for the Perplexed*.
Munk, 1, 26, 27, 49, 55.
Mutakallimun, 47-9, 55, 56, 62, 84, 91, 96.

Najimites, 51.
Narboni, 44, 67, 72, 73, 95, 98, 109.
Naturanschauung, 36.
Neumark, David, 39.
Newton, Isaac, 28, 73.

Olam Katan, see *Microcosm*.
Opinions. see *Emunot we-Deot*.
Or Adonai, 41, 67, 69, 75, 85, 89, 98, 104, 105, 107.

Palquera, 39.
Philo, 2.
Philosophie des Salomon ibn Gabirol, by Guttmann, 39.
Physics, by Aristotle, 5, 33, 55, 64, 65, 70, 88.

INDEX

Plato and the Older Academy, 4, 5, 11, 21, 27, 33, 64, 69, 70.
Platonische Studien, 5.
Prantl, 15.
Principes by Descartes, 34.
Problem der Materie in der griechischen Philosophie, 33.
Pseudo-Platonism, 33, 35, 38, 45, 46 *et seq.*
Psychologie bei den jüdischen Religionsphilosophen, 22, 26.
Psychologisches System des Maimonides, 36, 40.
Ptolemy, 63, 96.
Pythagoreans, 7.

Rab Pealim, 73, 98.
Raumtheorie im späteren Platonismus, 2.
Religionsphilosophie des Saadia, 92.
Renan, 1.
Ritter, 7.
Ruaḥ Ḥen, 37.

Saadya, 1, 28, 29, 49, 50, 53, 57, 62-4, 91.
Samuel ibn Tibbon, 36 *et seq.*
Saul, a pupil of del Medigo, 45.
Scharistani, 51.
Schechter, S., 28.
Scheyer, 36, 37, 40.
Schmiedl, 37, 39.
Schreiner, 49.
Sefer ha-Gedarim, 68.
Sefer Musar, 27.
Sefer Yesodat, 38, 49, 53.
Sefer Yeẓirah, 29, 64.
Sheelot Shaul ha-Cohen, 37, 39.
Shem Tob b. Shem Tob, 44, 105.

Simplicius, 69, 70.
Spinoza, 2, 93, 97, 101, 107.
Steinschneider, 2, 21, 67, 98, 105.
Studien über Religionsphilosophie, 37.

Tabrizi, 105, 107.
Thomas Aquinas, 86.
Timaeus, 5-9, 11.
Tractatus de Anima, 27.
Tree of Life, see *Eṣ Ḥayyim.*

Void, 71-81; Aristotle on, 17; Aristotelianism versus Kalam, 71; Jewish philosophy at first denies existence of, 72; Joseph ibn Zaddik follows Aristotle, 72; Maimonides and Ibn Latif on, 73; relative versus absolute void, 74; Gersonides's argument against, and his difficulty with the word 'beyond', 75 *et seq.*; Halevi on, 78; Crescas's reply to Gersonides and his refutation of the four Aristotelian arguments, 78-84; Abrabanel's reaction, 85; his evolutionary theory of the psychic finiteness, 86; summary of, 112-113.

Wars of God, see *Milḥamot Adonai.*
Works of God, see *Mif'alot Elohim.*

Yesod Olam, 50, 56, 99.

Zeller, 5-7, 11.
Zeno of Elea, 1, 4, 51-3, 57, 59, 64, 65, 84, 115.
Zifrinowitsch, 28.